D1373347

QUICK
STUDIES
Matthew & Mark

DAVID C. COOK PUBLISHING CO.
ELGIN, ILLINOIS—WESTON, ONTARIO

The following authors and editors contributed to this volume:

Stan Campbell
John Duckworth
Jim Townsend, Ph.D.

Quick Studies
Matthew and Mark

© 1992 David C. Cook Publishing Co.

Published by David C. Cook Publishing Co.
850 North Grove Ave., Elgin, IL 60120
Cable address: DCCOOK
Designed by Bill Paetzold
Cover illustrations by Steve Björkman
Inside illustrations by Paul Turnbaugh and Jack DesRocher
Printed in U.S.A.

ISBN: 0-7814-0025-2

MATTHEW

MARK

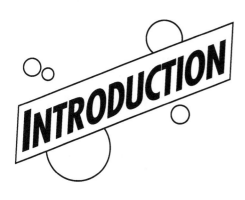

Quick Questions about Quick Studies

We've made *Quick Studies* as self-explanatory as possible, so you can dive in and start using them right away. But just in case you were wondering . . .

When should I use *Quick Studies*?

Whenever you want high school or junior high kids to explore the Bible face-to-face and absorb it into their lives. We've kept the openers active and the discussion questions creative, so you can use *Quick Studies* with confidence in Sunday school, midweek youth Bible study, small groups, even youth group meetings and retreats.

What's so quick about *Quick Studies*?

They're designed to save you preparation time. The session plans are compact, for quick reading. There aren't a lot of materials to gather, either (you'll need Bibles, pencils and paper, copies of the reproducible sheets, and sometimes a few other items). Yet *Quick Studies* are *real* Bible studies, with plenty of thought-provoking discussion and life application.

How are these different from other youth Bible studies?

We like to think *Quick Studies* are . . .

• *Irresistible.* You already know most kids don't jump at the chance to fill in a bunch of blanks in a boring study guide. So we used creative, reproducible sheets and *active* activities to draw kids into Scripture.

• *Involving.* You need discussion *starters*, not discussion *stoppers*. We avoided dull "yes or no" questions and included lots of thought-provokers that should get your group members talking about important issues. And we didn't forget suggested *answers* to most of the tougher questions, which should make things easier for you.

• *Inductive.* Many Bible studies try to force-feed kids a single "aim" and ignore other points Scripture is trying to make. *Quick Studies* let kids discover a variety of key principles in a passage.

• *Influential.* It's not enough to know what the Bible says. Every session includes a step designed to help kids decide what to do *personally* with vital points from the chapter.

When do kids read the passages covered?

That's up to you. If your group is into homework, assign the passages in advance. If not, take time to read the Scripture together after the "Opening Act" step that kicks off each session. There are dozens of ways to read a passage—with volunteers taking turns, or with a narrator and actors "performing" a scene, or with kids underlining points as they read silently, or with you reading as the author and kids listening as the original audience, or with small groups paraphrasing as they read . . .

What if I want to cover more—or less—than a chapter in a session?

Quick Studies is flexible. Each 45- to 60-minute session covers a chapter of the New Testament, but you can adjust the speed to fit your group. To cover more than one chapter in a session, just pick the points you want to emphasize and drop the activities, questions, and reproducible sheets you don't need. To cover less than a chapter, you may need to add a few questions and spend more time discussing the "So What?" application step in detail.

Do I have to cover a whole New Testament book?

No. Each session stands alone. Use sessions one at a time if you want to, or mix and match books in any order you choose. No matter how you use them, *Quick Studies* are likely to help your group see Bible study in a whole new light.

John Duckworth, Series Editor

Roots

After a long period of biblical history, the time is finally right for the birth of Jesus, the promised Messiah. Of course, the miracle of a virgin being "with child" causes no small commotion in the lives of Mary and Joseph, but angelic intercession helps Joseph understand what's going on.

Distribute the reproducible sheet, "Humble Beginnings." Ask kids to complete the quiz. Answers: 1(n); 2(e); 3(o); 4(k); 5(m); 6(h); 7(l); 8(b); 9(j); 10(i); 11(a); 12(f); 13(g); 14(d); 15(c). Discuss: **According to Matthew 1, what kind of earthly beginnings did Jesus have? What might most people expect from a person with His background and beginnings?**

DATE I USED THIS SESSION _____ GROUP I USED IT WITH _____

NOTES FOR NEXT TIME _____

_____

_____

1. The New Testament begins with the family tree of Jesus. Why do you think Matthew goes into such detail? (The birth of the Messiah had been promised and prophesied for hundreds of years. Also, Jewish people would be able to see that Jesus was a direct descendant of Abraham and David.)

2. Do you recognize anyone mentioned in the genealogy (vss. 2-16)? (A few names should be familiar. Like most of us, Jesus had a lot of relatives who seemed insignificant. Still, all were part of His "family tree.")

3. How is Joseph different from the other men mentioned (vs. 16)? (After a list of people who were "the father of" other people, Joseph was recorded as the husband of Mary rather than the father of Jesus. This reflects the fact that the Holy Spirit, not Joseph, brought about Mary's pregnancy.)

4. What was the marital status of Mary and Joseph when she became pregnant with Jesus (vs. 18)? (They were engaged, which in their time was much more binding than in our society.)

5. Would Mary's situation be a "public disgrace" (vs. 19) if it happened today? How would people in your school and church treat her?

6. How do you think Mary and Joseph felt about their situation? Act out two dinnertime conversations they might have had—one before and one after the angel talked to Joseph (vs. 20).

7. God's Son was to be named Jesus ("the Lord saves"— vs. 21). The people would call Him Immanuel ("God with us"—vs. 23). What name might you give to someone who would do the things Jesus did? Would one name be enough?

8. Since the birth of Jesus had been foretold by the prophets (vs. 22), would you expect people to be prepared for His birth? Do you think they actually were? Explain.

9. Joseph did as he was instructed (vs. 24). **Put yourself in his place. What kinds of comments do you think he might have received as Mary "started to show"?** (Perhaps teasing from coworkers; advice from family members to get rid of Mary, the silent treatment, etc.)

10. The Bible makes it clear that Joseph did not have sex with Mary before the birth of Jesus. **Why is this important?** (The virgin birth of Jesus fulfilled prophecy; it showed that He was literally the Son of God, etc.)

Many people think Mary was quite young when Jesus was born—maybe a teenager. God entrusted her with this major assignment. Ask kids:

• **What do you think you would have done in Mary's (or Joseph's) place? (a) Done what God wanted, even if it meant having everyone look down on you? (b) Come up with a good excuse not to do what He asked? (c) Tried a compromise?**

• **What are two things God might want you to do today that might be almost as challenging?**

• **Are you ready to do something major for God right now, or are you waiting until you're older? If so, how old?**

HUMBLE BEGINNINGS

Can you match

these celebrities

with their

"beginnings"?

_____ 1. Mickey Mouse

_____ 2. Abraham Lincoln

_____ 3. Madonna

_____ 4. Dr. Martin Luther King, Jr.

_____ 5. Teenage Mutant Ninja Turtles

_____ 6. Arnold Schwarzenegger

_____ 7. Michael Jackson

_____ 8. Mikhail Gorbachev

_____ 9. Sojourner Truth

_____ 10. Marilyn Monroe

_____ 11. David Letterman

_____ 12. Albert Einstein

_____ 13. Babe Ruth

_____ 14. Thomas Edison

_____ 15. Madame Curie

a. As a TV weatherman

b. Born in a village called Privolnoye

c. As a child with the last name of Sklowdowska

d. With only three months of formal education

e. Born on a farm in Kentucky

f. As a five-year-old impressed by a pocket compass

g. As a kid in Baltimore with the middle name Herman

h. As a skinny kid in Austria

i. As a girl named Norma Jean

j. As a slave named Isabella Baumfree

k. As the second child of a Georgia minister

l. As a local singer in Gary, Indiana

m. As a joke, making fun of comic book heroes

n. In the movie, *Steamboat Willie*

o. As a dancer living in a cockroach-infested apartment

MATTHEW 2

The Eastern Detectives

The young Jesus is visited by wise men from far away who bring Him gifts. Their public inquiry about His special nature alarms King Herod, who tries to have the young Christ put to death—murdering many babies in the process.

Before kids arrive, hide something of value (silver dollar, small stuffed animal, cassette tape, etc.) in the meeting area. Depending on the size of the object and the cleverness of your hiding place, you might also want to provide maps or clues. It's likely that the object will be found by someone who exerts a lot of effort. Keep this in mind later as you compare the Magi's effort to find Jesus with King Herod's effort.

DATE I USED THIS SESSION _____ GROUP I USED IT WITH _____

NOTES FOR NEXT TIME _____

_____

_____

1. This Gospel doesn't record many specifics of the birth of Jesus. But after He was born, He was visited by "Magi." What were they? (Probably astrologers or astronomers.)

2. Why would these "foreigners" care about the king of the Jews? (Maybe because they knew the prophecies about Him, which indicated He would do some amazing things.)

3. If you'd been one of the Magi, what might have irritated you most about your long journey? What would have kept you going?

4. When the Magi checked in with King Herod, why was he disturbed (vs. 3) to hear that there was "a new king in town"? (Herod was not from the line of David, and would have felt threatened by someone who had better credentials.)

5. If you'd been one of the Magi, would you have been suspicious about Herod's assignment (vs. 8)? Why or why not? (If Herod had really wanted to worship the child, he could have gone along. Bethlehem was only about five miles away.)

6. Play detective as you read verses 9-11. What clues can you find that suggest the Magi didn't stand around the manger with the shepherds, as many nativity scenes suggest? (Jesus is referred to as a "child" rather than a "baby," and the Magi found Him at a "house.")

7. Are the words of the carol, "We Three Kings," backed up by this passage? (No. Nowhere does the Bible say the men were kings. Nor does it say how many were present [though there were three kinds of gifts].)

8. Do you think there was any significance in the gifts of the Magi? (Some suggest gold represented the purity or royalty of Jesus, incense the pleasant aroma of His perfect life, and myrrh [a burial spice] His sacrificial death.)

9. Why do you think God directed the Magi from their faraway country to Bethlehem? (Perhaps since Jesus came to save the "world," it was logical to have "international" delegates present to celebrate His birth.)

10. **How do you feel about Herod's slaughter of all those babies? Does it "spoil" the Christmas story?** (This massacre *should* cause us pain. The Bible is reporting the facts, not telling a sweet story of candy canes and soft music. The birth of Jesus was an invasion into enemy territory, and the slaughter was an effort to keep Jesus from carrying out His mission. Note that Herod, a cruel man, also killed some of his own children and wives.)

11. **How might your life be different today if the child Jesus had not escaped to Egypt? If He had not moved to Nazareth?**

Hand out copies of "Finding and Giving," the reproducible sheet. Have kids fill out Part I. Discuss:

• **Do you think people don't find Jesus because He's well hidden, or because they aren't looking hard enough?**

• **If Jesus were appearing on earth today, how far would you go to see Him?**

• **If you've received Jesus, what are some of the "guiding lights" that helped you find Him? How could you be a "star" to someone else?**

• **The Magi traveled in a group. Do you feel *our* group is looking for Jesus together? How could we make it easier for you to find Jesus and His will?**

Then have students fill out Part II and share with the group the gifts they could offer Jesus. Try to use some of these gifts in your youth program as soon as possible.

Part I: Finding

The Magi went out of their way to find Jesus. They left behind their families, their studies, and everything else—with the sole purpose of finding God's promised Messiah.

How about you? Determine how strongly you agree with each of the following statements. (1 = Don't agree at all; 10 = Totally agree)

I have found Jesus and received Him as my Savior.	1 2 3 4 5 6 7 8 9 10
I try every single day to find Jesus' will for my life.	1 2 3 4 5 6 7 8 9 10
I like to know where Jesus is, but sometimes I don't like to get too close.	1 2 3 4 5 6 7 8 9 10
I think my search for Jesus will continue all my life.	1 2 3 4 5 6 7 8 9 10
Certain things in my life prevent me from seeking Jesus with all my heart.	1 2 3 4 5 6 7 8 9 10
I don't work too hard to find Jesus, but I hope He finds me.	1 2 3 4 5 6 7 8 9 10
Like the star, I'm guiding others to find Jesus.	1 2 3 4 5 6 7 8 9 10

Part II: Giving

The Magi gave Jesus valuable gifts. You may think, *Last time I checked, I didn't have a lot of gold, incense, or myrrh—or anything else of value.* Maybe not. But what *can* you offer Jesus as a gift? Perhaps you have a special talent. Maybe you have time to spend with other people. Maybe you have a voice that can sing or tell others about God. In the space below, describe or draw the gift(s) you would be willing to give Jesus.

Operation Desert Steamroller

John the Baptist begins his ministry of preparing the way for Jesus. He baptizes repentant people, warns the Pharisees of their improper attitudes, and reluctantly baptizes Jesus as He, too, prepares to begin public ministry.

Have students pair up. Explain that a press conference (imaginary) is being held because of public demand to determine the most important group member. The goal of each person is to introduce his or her partner as brilliantly as possible. Partners should be encouraged to gather facts from each other, but the "press" will be looking more at the style of the person giving the introduction. After everyone has had an opportunity to introduce someone, vote on who did the best job. Then later in the session, contrast that person's style to the approach used by John the Baptist.

DATE I USED THIS SESSION _____ GROUP I USED IT WITH _____

NOTES FOR NEXT TIME _____

_____

_____

1. If you were walking down the street and heard someone preaching, "Repent, for the kingdom of heaven is near" (vs. 2), what would you do?

2. What did John the Baptist mean when he said, "The kingdom of heaven is near"? (Scholars debate the precise meaning, but it was certainly a proclamation that people should get ready to receive Jesus. See also verse 3.)

3. The Jewish people anxiously awaited a kingdom ruled by the Messiah, but John was saying they had to repent (turn away from their sins) before they could enter this new kingdom. How do you think they felt about that?

4. How might people respond if John the Baptist showed up at your church to preach a sermon and attend a potluck dinner? If he spoke to your youth group for five minutes, what do you think he would say?

5. After hearing John, many people confessed their sins and were baptized (vss. 5, 6). What's the most public thing you've done to admit you've done something wrong, or to declare what you believe?

6. John lashed out at the religious leaders (vss. 7-10), calling them vipers, knocking their traditional claim to the kingdom (being descended from Abraham), etc. If these leaders had gone back to town and defended themselves in a letter to the local paper, what might they have written? Try your hand at such a letter.

7. If you'd been there, what would have been your biggest objection to being baptized? Would you have done it anyway?

8. How does John describe the man for whom he is preparing the way (vss. 11, 12)? (Powerful, bringing the Holy Spirit, ready to separate wheat from chaff, etc.) **From what you know of Jesus, how did He follow through on these predictions?** (He turned the religious leaders and the world upside-down, made eternal life possible, and sent the Holy Spirit to believers.)

9. If you'd been John the Baptist, how do you think you would have felt after Jesus finally appeared on the scene? Relieved? Disappointed? Confused about what to do next?

10. If God described you in a voice from heaven (vss. 16, 17), what do you think He might say? What would you want Him to say?

Distribute copies of "Paving the Way." Group members can work individually or in teams to come up with solutions. As needed, point out that most of the "bumps" could be smoothed if we were more consistent in following Jesus' example, and were more honest with our friends and families about the fact that Christians aren't perfect. Encourage kids to think of specific ways to "pave the road" this week for Jesus to enter a friend or relative's life.

PAVING THE WAY

John the Baptist was sort of a steamroller—paving the "road" for the arrival of Jesus. How about you? Are you smoothing out any bumps, preparing the way for Jesus to come into the lives of your friends and family? Or are you making the road rockier?

Take a look at the following "bumps"—attitudes that keep people from accepting Jesus. What could you do to smooth out these bumps, paving the way for people to think seriously about accepting Him?

BUMP	HOW TO SMOOTH IT OUT
"I saw you punch that guy who fouled you in the basketball game. Some Christian you are."	
"I feel perfectly fine without Jesus. You may need Him, but I don't."	
"I saw a movie about how Jesus was just like the rest of us, without any super powers or anything."	
"Christians don't care about people's real problems—like hunger and gangs."	
"Those TV evangelists are always asking for money."	
"If being a Christian is so great, how come you never said anything about it before?"	

MATTHEW 4

Don't Tempt Me

Immediately after Jesus is baptized, He enters the wilderness for a 40-day period of fasting. While there, He is tempted by the devil. After successfully withstanding Satan's temptations, Jesus begins to call disciples as He starts His public ministry.

(Needed: Loaf of bread)

Have kids stand in a circle. Toss around a securely wrapped loaf of bread. Name a person in the circle who, you say, "has the power to turn bread into stone." As the loaf is tossed, this person will turn the bread to stone simply by saying "Stone!" whenever he or she wishes. The person catching the loaf next must act as if he or she has been hit by a 100-pound boulder, and will be out. Name another person who has "the power to turn stone into bread." This person will do so by saying "Bread!" whenever he or she wishes, and the next one catching the loaf will be safe. If time allows, toss the bread until just one person is left; it should be the one who can change stone to bread, because he or she can always turn "incoming" stone to bread. Discuss how the two people with "super powers" felt. Ask why "showing off" your abilities is so tempting. Refer to this later when you discuss the temptation for Jesus to turn stone to bread.

DATE I USED THIS SESSION _____ GROUP I USED IT WITH _____

NOTES FOR NEXT TIME _____

_____

_____

1. Have you ever felt as if you were wandering in a spiritual wilderness, or as if you were being tested? What happened?

2. Why would the stone-to-bread transformation have been tempting to Jesus? (He'd just fasted for forty days.) If the devil wanted to hit a weak spot of yours, what would he tempt you to turn stones into?

3. What would have been so bad about turning stones to bread (vss. 1-4)? (It was an attempt to get Jesus to use His power for His own benefit, which was not what He had come to do.)

4. When Jesus refused to "test" God by throwing Himself off the temple (vss. 5-7), was it because He thought God wouldn't protect Him? Explain. (Testing God puts Him in the role of servant, following your orders. We are to follow His.)

5. Which of the following are "testing" God: A guy who keeps looking at pornography, figuring he can ask forgiveness each time; a girl who goes skydiving; a guy who drives a car that has worn-down brakes?

6. Do you think the third temptation (vss. 8-11) was (a) so obvious that Jesus would never fall for it; (b) bogus, because the devil couldn't deliver the whole world; or (c) the most tempting of the three? Why?

7. What was Jesus' reward for withstanding the temptations (vs. 11)? (He was attended by angels.) What are *our* rewards for resisting temptation? (Staying close to God, avoiding suffering in this life and punishment in the next, having God's approval, receiving a crown in heaven, etc.)

8. If you had a tape recording of Jesus saying the following, how do you think His voice would sound? "Repent, for the kingdom of heaven is near"; "Come, follow me, and I will make you fishers of men." What background noises might you hear on the tape?

9. What did Jesus do that caused word about Him to spread so quickly (vss. 23-25)? (He taught, told people about God's kingdom, and healed all kinds of diseases.) **What three things could you do to attract people to Jesus today? What three things could your group do?**

10. If you were living during this time and heard about Jesus, would you have tried to find Him to see what was going on? Why?

Hand out copies of "On the Tip of Your Tongue." This may be difficult for some, so follow up the individual exercise with a group brainstorming session. Follow with a challenge to face temptation as Jesus did—by knowing *what* the Bible has to say and *when* to put those teachings into action.

ON THE TIP OF YOUR Tongue

*E*ach time Jesus was tempted in the wilderness, He fought back by quoting a well-chosen passage of Scripture. Let's see how good you are at His method. For each of the temptations listed below, see how many Bible verses you can think of that would help you do the right thing.

1. Monday morning before school, a friend runs up to you and says, "You wouldn't believe how busy my weekend was. I didn't have time to do a lick of homework. Quick, let me see what you did for our English and math assignments. Don't worry; I won't copy them word for word."

_____

2. You're on a date. The other person is putting a lot of pressure on you to do more than you know you should do. When you begin to resist, he or she says, "C'mon, don't you really love me?"

_____

3. You're a football player. You've been determined not to drink alcoholic beverages. But your team has just won the state championship, and three of your friends are begging you to do some "serious" partying with them.

_____

4. Everyone always picks on Greg ("the Geek"). You don't think he's such a bad guy, but one day in the cafeteria everyone is giving him a hard time. It's obvious that they expect you to go along with them, and you *do* have a couple of clever insults that no one has heard yet. This would be an ideal time to use them, and you could apologize to Greg later, when no one else is around.

_____

5. You're a guy who's been grounded, but the cutest girl in school phones you and tries to persuade you to come over.

_____

6. You're a senior in high school. You're offered a once-in-a-lifetime job in the area of your major. As your prospective boss offers you the job, he explains that the company will pay for your college tuition. But he also expects you to work most Sundays and nights when your church usually meets.

_____

A FEW VERSES TO GET YOU STARTED

James 4:7
Psalm 119:9-11, 16
Exodus 20:3-17
Micah 6:8
I Corinthians 10:13
Philippians 3:13, 14
Philippians 4:8, 13

MATTHEW 5

The Greatest Sermon Ever Told, Part I

As Jesus begins to teach and heal the sick, He quickly gets the attention of the people in the surrounding areas. As crowds of eager listeners begin to gather, He goes onto a mountainside and begins to explain God's plan for a new and better way of life.

Play a game of Simon Says, but with a twist. Just before beginning, say, "Oh, by the way, during this game 'stand' means 'jump,' 'jump' means 'sit,' and 'sit' means 'stand.'" Then begin to give commands such as, "Simon says jump," "Simon says stand on one foot," etc. In addition to the challenge of doing only what Simon says to do, the matter is complicated by redefining basic terms. In this session kids will see that Jesus "redefines" terms such as murder and adultery. It may be difficult to do what God says while trying to adjust to the new definitions, but it's important that we keep working at it.

DATE I USED THIS SESSION _____ GROUP I USED IT WITH _____

NOTES FOR NEXT TIME _____

_____

_____

1. Read verses 1-12 and debate this question: Is Jesus setting up a religion for losers here? (Note that for every action Jesus lists that might be considered weak or vulnerable, He also provides a great promise. The "losers" in life are those who try to be self-sufficient instead of depending on God's power.)

2. Of the promises Jesus makes, which is most appealing to you? In the last week, how have you shown the attitude or action connected with that promise—or have you?

3. Have you ever been insulted, persecuted, or falsely accused of something because of your Christian beliefs (vs. 11)? If so, did you "rejoice and be glad" (vs. 12)? What reward do you look forward to in heaven because of your suffering?

4. What point is Jesus making by talking about unsalty salt and hidden light (vss. 13-16)? (People who are "Christian" in name only have no effect on others [no *positive* effect, at least]. But when we set an example so others will see Jesus reflected in us, we make a difference in the world.)

5. Based on Jesus' expanded definition of "murder" (vss. 21, 22), how many "murders" would you say take place each day on TV? In your school? In your home?

6. How could you keep from "murdering" someone with hate, based on Jesus' advice in verses 23-26? (Settle your disagreement before trying to worship God; start patching things up yourself instead of waiting for the other person; don't allow your conflict to drag out; remember that you're the one to suffer if you don't settle your disagreements.)

7. What bothers you most about verses 27-38? What do you think Jesus was really saying? (No short-term thrill is worth long-term separation from God. We may need to set tough restrictions on ourselves if nothing else seems to work. Jesus was not endorsing self-mutilation, but His statement shows us how serious lust is to God.)

8. How do you think the crowd reacted to verses 31, 32? How do you react?

9. Based on verses 33-37, what phrases and attitudes should be "bleeped out" of your everyday conversation? (Oaths like "by God"; any attempt to weasel out of a simple yes or no you've given, such as saying, "Well, I didn't *promise*.")

10. See verses 38-42. Do you think it takes a stronger person to "fight back," or to react as Jesus instructed? Why? (It takes a strong and disciplined person to turn the other cheek and not demand "justice" for every offense.)

11. How could Jesus' expanded definition of love (vss. 43-48) change a pep rally? A speech tournament? Your school cafeteria? Your youth group?

The reproducible sheet, "Radical Report Card" will help group members evaluate their behavior in light of this portion of the Sermon on the Mount. Follow with a discussion (without pressing) of what each person does best and worst, and encourage kids to help each other out in needed areas as well as hold each other accountable for improvement.

If some of your grades are low, try to think of some things you could do to bring them up.

Jesus taught some radical, new things in the Sermon on the Mount. People who heard Him probably compared what He said to the way they usually acted. We need to do that, too. So, for each of the following pairs of statements below, circle the letter grade closest to the statement that describes the way you usually act. The more you do what Jesus said (listed in the left-hand column), the higher your grade should be.

I'm "poor in spirit" (totally dependent on God)	A B C D F	I totally ignore God because I don't need Him
I'm able to mourn (because I know I need more help than I can provide for myself)	A B C D F	I laugh at others' problems and the idea of getting help from God
I'm meek (not "wimpy," but I keep my power under control)	A B C D F	I step on anyone who gets in my way
I'm hungry and thirsty for righteousness	A B C D F	I'm only into eating, drinking, and being merry
I show mercy	A B C D F	I never forgive
I'm pure in heart	A B C D F	I only pretend to be pure
I'm a peacemaker	A B C D F	I'm itching to fight
I'm persecuted (or insulted) because of my faith	A B C D F	I deny my faith to fit in
I'm "salty" (making a difference in a world without much flavor)	A B C D F	I try to sneak through life without making any difference for God
I let my light shine (doing good things to bring God glory)	A B C D F	I leave good deeds to the Boy Scouts and leave witnessing to preachers
I never murder (or use insults, name calling, etc.)	A B C D F	I wish I could kill somebody
I settle conflicts before they get out of hand	A B C D F	I hold grudges
I avoid adultery (also lusting, leering, gawking, etc.)	A B C D F	I store up fantasies and act on them
I avoid oaths (empty promises, swearing, etc.)	A B C D F	I say whatever I feel like saying
I turn the other cheek (not demanding justice or vengeance when offended)	A B C D F	I get even every time
I love my enemies	A B C D F	I see enemies as slime

MATTHEW 6

The Greatest Sermon Ever Told, Part II

Jesus continues His Sermon on the Mount by clarifying some of the things God expects as we worship. He explains that *what* we do can't be evaluated without also considering *why* we do it. The proper attitude is essential in anything we do in the Lord's name.

Have volunteers perform the skit, "The Hip O'Kritt Show" (found on the reproducible sheet). Or videotape it in advance and show it to the group. Then discuss: **What does it mean to be a hypocrite? How have you seen people say one thing and do another? How do we usually respond to hypocrites?** Later, discuss how easily God sees through our own insincere behavior. Worship is one thing we can't fake.

DATE I USED THIS SESSION _____ GROUP I USED IT WITH _____

NOTES FOR NEXT TIME _____

_____

_____

1. If you were caught doing an "act of righteousness" by a candid camera (vs. 1), what might it be? How could doing your giving, prayer, or fasting "for the camera" affect the way you do these things?

2. Check out verses 2-4. What do you think Jesus would say about TV evangelists who advertise the projects they want money for? About people who give mainly as a tax write-off? About those who give away only worn-out stuff? About people who frequently remind others that they tithe to the church? What would Jesus say about *your* giving?

3. When you pray (vss. 5-8), do you tend to be more public or private? Long-winded or brief? Repeating stock phrases or making it up as you go?

4. Do you think Jesus means that reciting the Lord's prayer every day (vss. 9-13) **will meet our "minimum daily requirement" for talking with God? Or does He expect more of us?** (The Lord's prayer is beautiful in its simplicity and shows that all prayers need not be long and complicated. However, it can also be used as an outline for more in-depth prayer. Suggest that group members focus on each phrase to spark other prayer concerns.)

5. Are our prayers for God's benefit, or for ours? Explain. (This is a trick question. God wants to hear our sincere praise and our concerns. But He is also ready to answer prayer and give us what we need. We should never try to limit prayer to what we get out of it, or to what we "owe" God. It should become a two-way communication.)

6. What's the connection between prayer and forgiveness (vss. 14, 15)? (We learn to forgive others as we keep experiencing God's forgiveness of our own sins.)

7. Jesus next talks about fasting, which is not as common a practice as it used to be. But His point is that we shouldn't act like martyrs when we do something a little special out of our love for God. What "spiritual" activities cause some kids to act like they're suffering? (When they "have" to sit through church, do chores or otherwise obey parents, visit a nursing home, etc.) **Why would the "martyr" act offend God?**

8. What **"treasures"** (vss. 19-21) **do you have stored in your house? What treasures do you have stored in heaven?**

9. What **"masters"** (vss. 22-24) **do you serve? How can you keep from being enslaved to these masters instead of serving God?** (Put Jesus above everything—jobs, school, family, etc. Only then can we see that He will keep all the other things in perspective.)

10. Think of someone who worries a lot (vss. 25-34). **Is that person fun to be around? Does the tendency to worry rub off on you? How do you keep from worrying about things you can't control?** (The things we can't control are never out of God's control.)

Have group members list every conceivable anxiety they deal with. Suggest categories like personal appearance, school, family, job, relationships, future, spiritual things, etc. Keep this brainstorming activity light. You might even impose a time limit and award a prize to the person with the most worries (such as a package of Rolaids or Pepto-Bismol). But after kids share some of their concerns, have them see what percentage of their worries are truly legitimate, and how many are somewhat hypocritical (not looking good, not having all the right clothes and possessions, etc.). Spend some time in discussion on how to keep from worrying so much about the wrong kinds of things.

THE HIP O' KRITT SHOW

Cast: Singers, Hip O'Kritt, Barney Baloney, Dr. Joyce Blathers

SINGERS *(to the tune of "Row, Row, Row Your Boat")*: Hip, Hip, Hip O'Kritt, welcome to his show; he's a lying phony and the biggest fake we know.

HIP: Hi, I'm Hip O'Kritt, and this is the Hip O'Kritt Show. And here's my sidekick, Barney Baloney.

BARNEY: You are correct, Hip!

HIP: What a great day! Even the smog tastes good! But seriously, let's talk about the homeless. I saw one while I was driving my Porsche. Or was it my Mercedes? Anyway, I care deeply about the homeless. And the environment, too. That's why I don't eat trees.

BARNEY: You are a great man, Hip!

HIP: Just a humble TV star, Barney! Now, who's our first guest today?

BARNEY: She's a doctor, Hip! Dr. Joyce Blathers!

HIP: She's great! A close personal friend! Let's bring her in! *(Applause)* Hi, Dr. Blunders.

DR.: That's Blathers. I'd like to conduct an experiment today, Hip. I'd like Barney to drink this *(holds up imaginary glass)*.

BARNEY: Sure! I'll drink anything! *(He drinks.)* What was that, Doc?

DR.: Truth serum. It makes you tell the truth, whether you want to or not.

HIP *(nervous)*: The truth? We don't do that stuff on this show.

BARNEY: I—I don't want to tell the truth!

DR.: See? It's working already.

HIP: Uh . . . Let's move on to our next guest. Who is it, Barney?

BARNEY: She's a terrible actress, Hip. No one has ever heard of her, but you told me to get her on the show because you want to go out with her.

HIP: You're not supposed to say that!

BARNEY: I can't help it. It's the truth serum.

HIP: Doc, you've got to make him stop! He'll wreck the show!

DR.: Sorry. It takes three hours to wear off.

BARNEY: Speaking of wear, Hip, that wig you wear is the worst I've ever seen. It looks like a dead possum is sitting on your head.

HIP: Barney, you're fired!

BARNEY: You can't fire me. I own this show. Remember, you sold it to me when you lost all your money gambling.

HIP: Aaaugh! You're ruining my career!

BARNEY: That's okay. I want Dr. Blathers to be the new host. She's nice.

DR.: Why, thank you, Barney. *(HIP starts sobbing.)* Looks like that's all the time we have today, folks. Cheer up, Hip. You could always go into advertising.

SINGERS *(again to the tune of "Row, Row, Row Your Boat")*: Hip, hip, hip, hooray! Hip is off the show! To tell the truth sincerely, we're all glad to see him go!

The Greatest Sermon Ever Told, Part III

Jesus concludes His Sermon on the Mount with a number of comparisons for us to consider: helpful criticism versus hypocritical judgment, narrow gate versus wide gate, good tree versus bad tree, house on rock versus house on sand, etc. His teachings amaze the people because He speaks with an authority that their religious leaders have never had.

Using the reproducible sheet, "Tell It to the Judge," have your group act out and debate the two cases—in the style of TV shows like *The People's Court,* if possible. Take a vote to determine the judge's rulings. Then make the transition from legal judgments to the *personal* judgments many of us make. Discuss how the parties in the two cases judged each other.

DATE I USED THIS SESSION _____ GROUP I USED IT WITH _____

NOTES FOR NEXT TIME_____

_____

_____

1. When it comes to judging people (vss. 1, 2), **do you tend to be lenient, or more of a "hanging judge"? Explain.**

2. When Jesus was talking about people with planks in their eyes (vss. 3-5), **do you think He was being solemn and serious, or do you think He said it somewhat tongue-in-cheek? Can you think of an example from your own life to illustrate the point He was trying to get across?**

3. Jesus spoke of pigs with pearls and sacred things at the mercy of dogs (vs. 6). **What do you think He meant?** (The good news of God's kingdom that He had come to proclaim was priceless and needed to be heard by receptive listeners. Some people are not ready to listen, and we should spend our time wisely, where we *can* make a difference.)

4. The idea of God as a Father was new to Jesus' listeners. **What kind of Father did Jesus describe in verses 7-11? Have you found God to be this kind of Father, or are you taking someone else's word for it?** (God the Father promises to provide for and "open the door" to His children. He desires that we come to Him and let Him know what we need.)

5. We learn the Golden Rule (vs. 12) **and repeat it without thinking much about it. But why did Jesus say it was so important?** (It pretty much sums up everything that was written in the Old Testament.)

6. If God is a Father who wants us to come to Him, **why do you think only a few people find the "narrow gate" (vss. 13, 14)?** (The decision to follow Jesus is an individual choice; many choose to follow the "broad" way, which seems to offer more instant rewards.)

7. We're not to be judgmental (vs. 1), **but we aren't to close our eyes to people who might intentionally mislead us** (vss. 15-20). **Can you think of any "ferocious wolves" "in sheep's clothing" you need to watch out for? How can you avoid being fooled by them?** (Many cults, for example, try to recruit followers or funds using the guise of Christianity. Yet a close examination usually reveals them for what they truly are. Knowing what's true helps you reject what's phony.)

8. **According to Jesus, the right words won't get you into heaven. Neither can you "perform" your way into the kingdom** (vss. 21-23). **So what's the secret?** (Each person's profession of faith must be accompanied by the willingness to seek and follow God's will.)

9. **Christianity is not just a "key" to get us into heaven. How else do we benefit from a relationship with Jesus?** (Vss. 24-27—It helps us keep going throughout the "storms" of life.) **What are some storms you're facing right now?**

10. Jesus amazed His listeners with His authority (vss. 28, 29). **Are *you* convinced that Jesus is a one-of-a-kind teacher? Is He just another authority figure to you? Is He one of several teachers whose writings you want to study? What do you think?**

Read verses 24-29 and ask: **Which of the following describes the foundation of your life? Option 1 is the House on the Sand. It's an accident waiting to happen. When the winds and rains hit, it's going to be a big pile of splinters. Option 2 is the Halfway House. This house is built on Jesus, yet the owner is so fond of the beach that he can't bear to part with certain "sandy" things that weaken the foundation. This house will survive more storms than the first, but sooner or later it will fall. Option 3 is the House on the Rock. This house is built on Jesus alone. It resists wind, rain, hail, hurricanes, monsoons, and termites.** Give kids time to reflect on this, especially on "sandy" attitudes or habits that may be weakening their foundations.

Tell It to the JUDGE

The Case of the Battered Bicycle

☞ The Plaintiff Says:

"I've known the defendant for about five years. We've been friends, more or less. Until now. I let this guy ride my bike just to try it out. It's a brand new ten-speed, metallic blue. He said he'd take it down to the gas station and back, about half a mile. Turns out he rode it about three miles, which I could tell from the odometer. When he came back, there was a big scrape along the side of the bike! This jerk ruined it! He was probably showing off when it happened. The bike shop says it'll need about $60 worth of work. I want my money, and I never want to see this geek again."

☞ The Defendant Says:

"I just wanted to try the bike out. It rode great—and it still does, even with a little scrape, by the way. I went three miles instead of one because there was a patch of fresh oil on the road to the station, and I had to go out of the way to keep from getting oil on the bike. The scrape wasn't my fault. This truck practically ran me off the road, and I slid into a chain link fence. Instead of being glad that I didn't get killed, this bozo says I have to pay him sixty bucks. I haven't got that kind of money. I will be looking for a new friend, though."

☞ The Judge Says:

The Case of the Permanent Promise

☞ The Plaintiff Says:

"I went to the beauty salon to get a permanent. Their guarantee on the wall said I'd get my money back if I wasn't satisfied. Well, I wasn't! The girl who did my hair was so busy answering the phone that she wasn't paying attention. She actually burned my hair! I could smell it! And the permanent looks awful. Besides frying my hair, she made the curls too tight. When I told her I wanted my money back, she said that only applied to the "deluxe" styling, which cost more. What a ripoff! After I get my money, I'm going to tell everybody I know to never go near that place."

☞ The Defendant Says:

"I'm sorry she wasn't satisfied. But the small print at the bottom of the sign does say that the guarantee only applies to the deluxe styling, which she didn't want. I did have to answer the phone a lot that day, but that doesn't mean I wasn't paying attention. She may have had one or two hairs burned, but it was probably the chemicals she smelled, not burning hair. Frankly, I think the real reason she wants her money back is because the permanent doesn't make her look like a movie star. I get so tired of people who come in here thinking we do magic. She's one of them."

☞ The Judge Says:

MATTHEW 8

It's a Miracle!

As he performs a number of miracles, Jesus demonstrates the omnipotent power of God—over disease, over time and space, over nature, and over the powers of Satan. Yet He makes it clear that following Him involves certain expectations in addition to receiving the benefit of His power.

Discuss the following questions taken from *The Book of Questions* (Gregory Stock, Ph.D., Workman Publishing, New York, © 1985, 1987).

• Would you accept $1,000,000 to leave the country and never set foot in it again?

• Would you accept twenty years of extraordinary happiness and fulfillment if it meant you would die at the end of the period?

• Would you be willing to have horrible nightmares for a year if you would be rewarded with extraordinary wealth?

Faced with all-or-nothing decisions, kids may find it hard to choose. Point out that following Jesus is an all-or-nothing choice that involves both benefits and sacrifice.

DATE I USED THIS SESSION _____ GROUP I USED IT WITH _____

NOTES FOR NEXT TIME_____

_____

_____

1. Put yourself in the place of the leper (vss. 1-4). **How do you think you would feel about your body? About other people? What would you be willing to do to be healed of your disease?** (In addition to the other consequences, lepers were "unclean" from a religious point of view, and unable to associate with "clean" people.)

2. **When you want something from God, are you as honest as this leper was? In what ways has Jesus "touched" you recently?**

3. **How are you like the centurion mentioned in verses 5-13? How are you different?** (Point out his power [centurions commanded more than 100 Roman soldiers], his concern, his understanding of the abilities of Jesus, and his great faith.)

4. **In verses 11 and 12, Jesus makes some bold statements. Do you think His words are positive or negative? Why?** (The good news is that Gentiles [non-Jews] will be welcomed into God's kingdom. The bad news is that so many people will reject Him.)

5. **When Jesus healed Peter's mother-in-law (vss. 14, 15), she immediately began to wait on Him. But what about all the others He healed (vss. 16, 17)? Do you think many of them stuck around to offer help? What do you think you would have done? Why?**

6. **Was Jesus trying to talk people out of following Him (vss. 18-22)? Why do you think He sounded so harsh?** (True discipleship involves real, lifelong commitment. It's not for everyone, and Jesus probably didn't want "followers" who hadn't thought through the consequences of their decisions.)

7. **How long do you suppose the disciples in the boat endured the storm before waking Jesus up (vss. 23-27)? Act out the conversation they might have had before waking Him.**

8. **Have you ever been in a scary situation with no assurance of being rescued? How did you respond? How did you "escape"?**

9. How is the account of demon possession in verses 28-34 different from "Hollywood" descriptions of demonic activity? What does this account tell you about the power of the devil and the power of God? (God is clearly much more powerful than Satan.)

10. Why did the townspeople beg Jesus to leave? (They may have been angry about the financial loss of their herd of pigs; they may also have feared His power. Either way, they didn't want Him to change their way of life.) **If Jesus appeared at your school, would he be asked to leave? Why or why not? If He appeared in your room at home, how long would you want Him to stay?**

The reproducible sheet, "Sticker Shock," will help kids consider the benefits and costs of following Jesus. Discuss: **Are the benefits worth the costs? Can you receive the benefits without paying the costs? Do any of the costs ever become benefits? Do you think Jesus is too demanding? What does He want from you that you find hardest to give?**

STICKER SHOCK

BRAND NEW LIFE LX

FIREBOUND UNCONVERTIBLE

Have you really thought about the benefits and costs of belonging to Jesus? How about the benefits and costs of *not* belonging to Him? If these two ways of life were cars, their stickers might look like this. Fill in the blanks with some ideas of your own. Then sign your name on one "Bottom Line" to show which way of life you choose. Remember—it's got to be one or the other!

Narrow Way Motors, Inc.
BRAND NEW LIFE LX

STANDARD FEATURES
- ✓ No guarantee of comfort
- ✓ Must make Christ top priority
- ✓ Access to His power over Satan/evil
- ✓ Access to His power over nature
- ✓ Eternity with God
- ✓ Persecution
- ✓ Forgiveness

_____
_____
_____

OPTIONS AVAILABLE
Help when you're in trouble
Help when you're sick
Martyrdom
Closeness to God
Joy

_____
_____

THE BOTTOM LINE

_____

Broad Way Motors, Inc.
FIREBOUND UNCONVERTIBLE

STANDARD FEATURES
- ✓ Flexible morals
- ✓ Not having to go to church
- ✓ Set your own priorities
- ✓ Not having to read the Bible
- ✓ Not having to serve others
- ✓ Eternity without God

_____
_____
_____

OPTIONS AVAILABLE
Wealth
Fame
Pleasure
Guilt
Power over people

_____
_____
_____

THE BOTTOM LINE

_____

MATTHEW 9

He's Got the Power

As Jesus continues to heal the sick, teach, and call disciples, He begins to draw criticism from the Pharisees and suspicion from the disciples of John the Baptist. Yet it's apparent that no question is too difficult for Him to answer and no problem is too large for Him to remedy.

(Needed: Nine books or magazines)

Before beginning, set up a "mind reading" demonstration with one other student or group leader. Lay out nine books or magazines in a 3 x 3 grid. Your partner leaves the room while the rest of the group chooses one of the magazines, then returns. Using a pointer, you ask, "Is this the one we have chosen?" When you get to the chosen one, your partner always says "yes." The trick is that as you point to the first magazine, you envision it in nine sections, just as the magazines are laid out; you point to the section that reveals the position of the chosen magazine. Repeat until some of the kids begin to catch on. Use this activity to show how we suspect a "trick" behind every "supernatural" talent. Just think of the confusion when Jesus showed that He could even raise people from the dead!

Pass out copies of the reproducible sheet, "Censored!" Have kids scan the chapter and follow the instructions on the sheet. Then discuss.

DATE I USED THIS SESSION _____ GROUP I USED IT WITH _____

NOTES FOR NEXT TIME _____

_____

_____

1. Suppose you're paralyzed. At last you're taken to Jesus, the one person in the world who can help you (vss. 1-8). He looks down on the mat where you're lying and says, "Take heart, your sins are forgiven." How do you feel? Do you want the disease cured or your sins forgiven? Why?

2. Why do you think Jesus used such a roundabout method of healing the paralyzed man? (Maybe He wanted to show the religious leaders that His power to heal was only a reflection of His power to forgive sins.)

3. Jesus called Matthew, a hated tax collector, to follow Him. What people are looked down on in your school, and what might happen if one of them tried to follow you around?

4. The first thing Matthew did was throw a party (vs. 10). Have you ever celebrated the privilege of following Jesus? If so, how?

5. Look at verses 9-13. Do you ever associate with certain people (for good reasons), only to receive criticism from others? Give some examples.

6. What does all this about patches and wineskins mean (vss. 14-17)? (Jesus was bringing a new way of life, not a slight change in the old way.) How could you make the same point using cars and paint jobs? Radios and cable TV?

7. What is the most you've ever trusted Jesus? Do you think you could have walked up to Him and asked Him to bring a dead relative back to life (vss. 18-25)? Explain.

8. No matter what Jesus did (vss. 18-33), the Pharisees wouldn't believe He was sent from God (vs. 34). How do some people today try to explain away His miracles? (By saying He was some kind of advanced scientist; that the Bible account isn't true; that the people He helped weren't really that sick, etc.)

9. What kind of workers was Jesus looking for (vss. 35-38)? How could you be a "shepherd" to a younger sister who is very shy? To an elderly person who lives alone? To a longtime friend who doesn't believe in Jesus?

Jesus did a lot of "impossible" things in this chapter. What do you need Him to do in your life? On a sheet of paper, list a few problems you can ask Him to solve. These could be "paralysis" problems—those that cause you to "freeze up" and not take action when you know you should. They might be "blindness" problems—those you can't see any answer for. Or they might be "deafness" problems—ones you could handle if you could just hear a word of encouragement or some ideas. Let kids share answers if they wish; if possible, remember these prayer concerns in future meetings.

Jesus took a boat back to His own town. A paralyzed man was brought to Him. Jesus said to the man, **CENSORED!**

This made the religious teachers very angry. Jesus was able to tell what they were **CENSORED!**

Then Jesus told the paralyzed man, **CENSORED!** The man **CENSORED!** The crowd was amazed.

Jesus asked Matthew to follow Him, which Matthew did. When Jesus had dinner with "sinners" at Matthew's house, the Pharisees got mad. Jesus replied that he had come to call sinners, not the righteous.

John's disciples asked Jesus why His disciples didn't fast. He said they would fast later, when He was taken from them.

A ruler with a sick daughter asked Jesus to heal her. Jesus was on His way to the man's house when a woman with a chronic bleeding problem touched Jesus' cloak, hoping to be healed. Jesus then **CENSORED!**

Meanwhile, the sick daughter had died. But Jesus went into her house and **CENSORED!**

Two blind men asked Jesus to heal them. He touched their eyes and they were **CENSORED!** He told them not to tell anyone, but they did anyway.

Then a man who was demon-possessed and couldn't talk was brought to Jesus. Jesus **CENSORED!** Again the crowd was amazed and the Pharisees were angry.

Jesus went through a number of towns, teaching and preaching and **CENSORED!** He had compassion on the people because they were like sheep who needed a shepherd.

MATTHEW 10

Go, Team!

After Jesus puts together his team of twelve disciples, He prepares to send them into the world with words of encouragement—and warning.

Ask small groups to act out the following scenes:

• A coach giving a pep talk to a team that's at the bottom of its league

• A mother talking to her beauty contestant daughter, who's just discovered a pimple on her nose ten minutes before the pageant starts

• A principal giving a "school spirit" speech to a student body whose school has just burned down

After the skits, discuss the importance of encouraging words at crucial times—which leads into the next section of the session.

DATE I USED THIS SESSION _____ GROUP I USED IT WITH _____

NOTES FOR NEXT TIME _____

_____

_____

1. Jesus' original disciples were given authority over evil spirits, disease, and death (vss. 1, 8). What authority do you think He has given you? (Be ready to share your or your church's view. Some feel Christians have a great deal of authority; others believe that only those with specific spiritual gifts can claim such power. But all Christians are promised help in overcoming evil, answers to prayer, wisdom during hard times, and the privilege of representing Jesus in the world.)

2. What can you tell about Jesus from His choice of disciples (vss. 2-4)? (He calls all kinds of people. He's not looking for just one type.)

3. What do you like best about the idea of being a disciple? Least?

4. How does Jesus want His disciples to develop trust in Him (vss. 9-13)? (By not accumulating a lot of money or possessions; by depending on "worthy" people to take them in; by facing regular rejection, etc.)

5. How can you love your enemies *and* "shake the dust off your feet" (vs. 14) if people won't listen? (It doesn't take a lot of time or energy to show love. But if a person does not want to become a Christian, we can devote our time to someone who does.)

6. How can you be "as shrewd as snakes *and* as innocent as doves" (vs. 16)? (Being innocent doesn't mean shutting down our brains. We should be thoughtful, observant, and practical [shrewd] so that others don't deceive us.) **How could you be shrewd and innocent if a gang member tried to recruit you?**

7. Do you think Jesus wants us to be persecuted for Him? Do you think He expects us to? (He tells us to flee to another place when persecuted [vs. 23]. Yet He knows that since He was persecuted, we will be, too.)

8. If we are like Jesus, we will suffer as He did (vss. 24, 25). But if we are like Jesus, what *positive* things can we

expect? (Vss. 26-33—Knowledge that nothing can harm us, at least not at a spiritual level [vs. 28]; assurance that God knows us intimately [vs. 30]; Jesus as our partner as we stand before God the Father [vs. 32], etc.)

9. **How does verse 28 make you feel? Confident? Frightened? Uncertain?**

10. **Do verses 34-36 sound like Jesus? Didn't He come to bring peace?** (Receiving Jesus certainly can bring inner peace, and peace with other believers. But division is unavoidable between those who trust Jesus and those who don't—even between family members.)

11. **How have you taken your cross** (vs. 38)? **How have you lost your life** (vs. 39)? **How have you given a cup of cold water** (vs. 42) **to someone who follows Jesus? What could be your next opportunity to do one of these?**

Hand out copies of the reproducible sheet, "Real Disciples." Have kids follow the instructions. Then discuss Part I, letting kids defend their answers (which probably will vary). Discuss Part II as kids are willing. Ask: **Do you think of yourself as a real disciple? Do you think God sees you that way? If you're not a real disciple, what are you?**

REAL DISCIPLES

Part I
Check the boxes that you think apply.

Real disciples don't . . .

- ❏ Drive cars.
- ❏ Go to school.
- ❏ Wear rollerblades.
- ❏ Stay quiet about their faith.
- ❏ Care about the poor.
- ❏ Go out on dates.
- ❏ Live in trailer parks.
- ❏ Get incurable diseases.
- ❏ Go into politics.
- ❏ Make fun of their parents.

Real disciples do . . .

- ❏ Smell like fish.
- ❏ Wear sandals.
- ❏ Have fun.
- ❏ Pray for their friends.
- ❏ Look forward to seeing Jesus.
- ❏ Obey God even when it hurts.
- ❏ Deny that they know Jesus.
- ❏ Turn normal people off.
- ❏ Stay away from non-Christians.
- ❏ Smile all the time.

Part II
Complete these sentences.

I felt most like a real disciple when . . . _____

The thing that scares me most about being a real disciple is . . . _____

One person I know who is a real disciple is . . . _____

This week I could be a real disciple by . . . _____

Let's Hear It for John

As Jesus travels around, teaching and preaching, He has a talk with the disciples of John the Baptist to confirm that He is the one John has prepared the way for. Jesus also pays tribute to John's faithfulness and contrasts it to others who had heard the Gospel message but were not responding to it.

Have a debate on the topic, "Resolved: Our city (or town or county) is the pits." Let kids form their own teams, or assign them to teams. You might want to act as moderator, with another leader or an "impartial" student as judge of which team does the better job. This activity will tie in to Jesus' condemnation of the cities that heard His teaching but didn't respond.

DATE I USED THIS SESSION _____ GROUP I USED IT WITH _____

NOTES FOR NEXT TIME _____

_____

_____

1. John the Baptist had faithfully proclaimed the coming of the Messiah. But after being in prison for awhile and not seeing Jesus become a popular political figure, he wasn't sure Jesus was the right guy (vss. 1-3). **Do you ever have any doubts about Jesus—even while you're going through all the right motions of Christianity? What kind?**

2. Based on Jesus' response to John (vss. 4-6), **how might you handle doubts when you have them?** (Look around and see God at work—in creation, in answered prayer, in hope that other people have for the future, etc.)

3. Jesus began His description of John the Baptist by saying what John *wasn't* (vss. 7, 8—a reed to be swayed by the wind or a wealthy, well-dressed man). **If Jesus were to describe you by what you *aren't*, what might He say?**

4. Jesus said John was a prophet (vss. 9-15), the "Elijah" predicted to come before the Messiah (Malachi 4:5). But since Jesus wasn't being accepted as Messiah, John wasn't being accepted as "Elijah." **What popularity or recognition could you lose because of your association with Jesus? How do you feel about that?**

5. You just can't please some people, according to Jesus (vss. 16-19). **How do you think He looked and sounded when he said these things? What was He talking about?** (John's serious nature caused him to be accused of demon possession, but the same people saw Jesus' social interactions and accused Him of gluttony and drunkenness.) **How is this like disagreements over what to do in your youth group? In your church?**

6. See verses 20-24. **How would you have felt if you lived in one of these cities? What might Jesus say about your town today?**

7. See verses 25, 26. **How does your view of Jesus today compare to the view you had as a preschooler? A fourth grader? Does it get harder or easier to believe as you get older?**

8. Why is your relationship with Jesus so important? (Vs. 27—Among other things, He's the only way to know God the Father.)

9. Since Jesus promises a lighter load (vss. 28-30), **why give us a "yoke" at all? Why doesn't He just take care of everything and let us have a good time?** (Dealing with problems can help us become more Christlike. Trying to take care of them ourselves makes the burden heavy. Trusting Jesus to see us through greatly lessens the load; that's how we find peace and rest.)

Hand out copies of the "Emergency!" reproducible sheet. Let group members think through how they would handle the situations listed. Then point out: **Some crises are obvious, and we know we have to act. But others are more subtle. For instance, it's easy to forget that people need to know about Jesus and eternal life. If we don't tell our friends, how will they find out? If we ignore them, how are we any better than the cities that soaked in all the teachings and miracles of Jesus, but didn't respond to His message?** Encourage kids to think of specific friends who need their spiritual "first aid."

Emergency

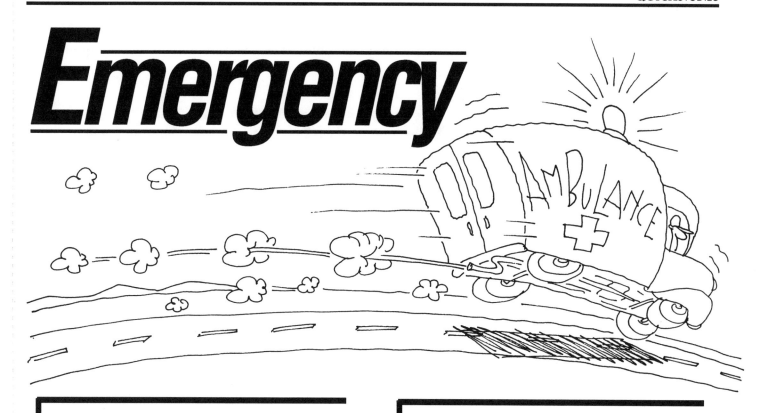

1. You're horseback riding in the country when you come across a car that has gone off the road, rolled over a couple of times, and smashed into a large tree. The driver is conscious, but just barely. She is bleeding from wounds in her forehead and right shoulder, but the bleeding doesn't seem too severe. The nearest home you can remember seeing was a couple of miles back, and there are no phones or other people around. It's up to you. What do you do?

2. A rumor is going around that Marc, a guy in your class, is selling drugs. You've heard this from several people, but have no evidence. Marc seems like a normal enough guy, but you don't know him well. After school you see him on a corner of the parking lot, talking to your 12-year-old neighbor— a nice (but somewhat insecure) kid named Barry. It seems Barry is giving Marc money, but they're too far away for you to be sure. What do you do?

3. Your best friend has been going through some incredibly rough times— parents' divorce, failing a required course, and not making the swimming team, to name a few. This person swears you to secrecy before telling you, "I can't take any more. I've got a gun, and I'm going to end it all tonight. I just wanted you to know." What do you do?

4. You're supposed to drop off some groceries for an elderly lady down your street, but there's no answer when you ring her doorbell. You know she can't be out. Then you see smoke coming from her kitchen window. All the doors and windows are locked. What do you do?

5. A close friend of yours is one of the most popular kids at school. He's good-looking, athletic, smart. But he feels no need for God. After all, things are going so well. What do you do?

Everybody's a Critic

The Pharisees begin to get really nit-picky about Jesus' actions, questioning His right to nibble on fresh-picked grain or heal on the Sabbath, and accusing Him of being in league with Beelzebub. But Jesus answers all their questions and continues to encourage people to seek the will of God.

Using the game board on the reproducible sheet, play "The Potshot Game." Provide a copy for every three or four kids. Have them flip coins to see how many spaces to move—one for heads, two for tails. Play until a few people reach the finish, if time allows. Then discuss: Did you notice anything unusual about this game? (As in life, the critical statements set you back a lot further than the compliments advance you.) **How do sincere compliments make you feel? How much criticism does it take to counteract praise?** Note that even Jesus, the perfect Son of God, received criticism He didn't deserve. We can expect the same.

DATE I USED THIS SESSION _____ GROUP I USED IT WITH _____

NOTES FOR NEXT TIME_____

_____

_____

1. Do you (or did you ever) have any rules about what you can't do (or must do) on Sundays? What do you think about them?

2. Do you think the Pharisees were really concerned that Jesus' disciples were nibbling on grain picked on the Sabbath (vss. 1-7)? **If not, what was their real motive for complaining?** (They wanted to find a way to keep Jesus from being so influential. They looked for chances to accuse Him of wrongdoing.)

3. Do you know people who, like the Pharisees, enjoy trying to get others into trouble? Why do you think they are that way? (Often such behavior reflects jealousy, so we shouldn't automatically get upset.)

4. What do you think Jesus meant when He referred to Himself as "Lord of the Sabbath" (vs. 8)? (The Sabbath had been set apart to honor God, and Jesus is God. He had the right to ignore the Pharisees hair-splitting rules.) **If Jesus appeared in this room right now, what might He remind us that He is Lord of?**

5. The Pharisees made their rules more important than relieving people's suffering (vss. 9-14). **What excuses keep us from helping people who suffer? What do you think Jesus would say about our excuses?**

6. When Jesus was able to answer every question the Pharisees asked, they plotted to kill Him (vs. 14). Why wouldn't they just admit He was right? Which is hardest for you to admit that Jesus is right about—prayer, possessions, or premarital sex?

7. Jesus kept telling people not to say He had helped them (vss. 15-21). **Why?** (The conflict with the Pharisees would eventually lead to His death. Though He had come to earth to die, He still had teaching and healing to do.)

8. If you had been a Pharisee, what in verses 25-37 would have made you most angry? What would have left you most confused? What might have kept you from yelling at Jesus or trying to punch Him?

9. When the Pharisees wanted to see a miracle, Jesus referred them back to Scripture (vss. 38-42). **What kinds of "signs" do people want from God today?** (A bolt of lightning, a rainbow, a voice, etc.) **Have you ever wished God would give you a sign? How could reading your Bible have done more good than seeing a "miracle"?**

10. According to Jesus (vss. 43-45), **is eliminating evil from your life enough to bring you close to God? Why not?**

11. If you're a member of Jesus' "family" (vss. 46-50), **do you feel like His brother or sister, son or daughter, or distant cousin? Why?**

Note that Jesus dealt with criticism by answering His critics with logic (vss. 25-28) and action (vss. 22, 23). Have kids look at "The Potshot Game" again to see how they could answer the criticisms in a similar way. You might also have them look up encouraging verses like Romans 8:1, 28, 31, 37-39; Philippians 4:4-8; and I John 4:4 that could help them combat the effects of destructive criticism.

THE POTSHOT GAME

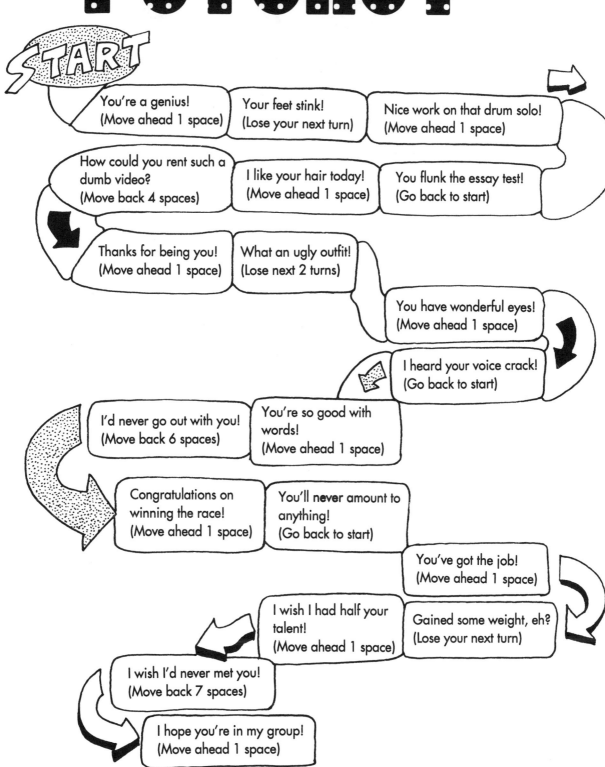

START

You're a genius!
(Move ahead 1 space)

Your feet stink!
(Lose your next turn)

Nice work on that drum solo!
(Move ahead 1 space)

How could you rent such a dumb video?
(Move back 4 spaces)

I like your hair today!
(Move ahead 1 space)

You flunk the essay test!
(Go back to start)

Thanks for being you!
(Move ahead 1 space)

What an ugly outfit!
(Lose next 2 turns)

You have wonderful eyes!
(Move ahead 1 space)

I heard your voice crack!
(Go back to start)

I'd never go out with you!
(Move back 6 spaces)

You're so good with words!
(Move ahead 1 space)

Congratulations on winning the race!
(Move ahead 1 space)

You'll **never** amount to anything!
(Go back to start)

You've got the job!
(Move ahead 1 space)

I wish I had half your talent!
(Move ahead 1 space)

Gained some weight, eh?
(Lose your next turn)

I wish I'd never met you!
(Move back 7 spaces)

I hope you're in my group!
(Move ahead 1 space)

Watch where you're going, stupid!
(Go back to start)

Finish

MATTHEW 13

Tales from the Light Side

Jesus begins to teach using parables. He refers to things that people are familiar with—seeds and soils, weeds, yeast, fishing nets, and so forth. While the people don't always know what He's talking about, He attracts large crowds who want to listen.

(Needed: Assorted common objects and optional prize)

Give each person a common object, such as a light bulb, golf ball, pencil, coin, etc. Each person is to create a story about the object. (The object might have parents, brothers and sisters, adventures, hopes, dreams, etc.) Have group members tell their stories; award a prize for the most imaginative if you like. Then explain that Jesus also used common objects to tell stories—though His taught spiritual truths.

DATE I USED THIS SESSION _____ GROUP I USED IT WITH _____

NOTES FOR NEXT TIME _____

1. What's your favorite story? Why do you like it more than all the others you've heard?

2. In Jesus' story of the sower (vss. 1-9), **what do** *you* **think He was trying to say? Compare your opinion with His explanation** (vss. 18-23).

3. From the devil's point of view, who are the heroes in the sower story? What "thorns" might he find most effective in "choking" you?

4. Why didn't Jesus just come right out and say what He meant? Why did He use parables? (Vss. 10-15—People usually listen better to stories than to sermons, and parables require a certain spiritual understanding before we can "interpret" the hidden meaning.)

5. In verse 12 Jesus says if you have something, you get a lot more of it, and if you don't have much, it's taken away from you. What do you think of that? (Some effort and knowledge are required for understanding spiritual things. People who make that effort will add to their understanding. Those who make only a half-hearted attempt to be "religious" will never really comprehend deep truths about God.)

6. How is the parable of the weeds (vss. 24-30) **like the parable of the net** (vss. 47-50)?

7. Which parables in this chapter have a happy ending? Which don't? Which might be too scary for a small child?

8. What do you think Jesus was teaching with His **parables of the mustard seed** (vss. 31, 32) **and the yeast** (vss. 33-35)? (These parables aren't explained, but perhaps they point out that certain things—whether faith or the kingdom of God—may start out small but grow to be very powerful.)

9. The parables of the hidden treasure and the pearl (vss. 44-46) **are a little easier to figure out. How would you exchange** *all* **you have to discover and obtain the kingdom of heaven? What things are you least willing to exchange?**

10. When Jesus asked the disciples if they understood all these things (vss. 51, 52), they said yes. Do you think they really understood? Why do people claim to understand spiritual things when they don't? What's one thing about God that you wish you understood better?

11. The place Jesus received least respect was in His hometown (vss. 53-58). **People there had known Him as a kid and didn't believe He was anybody special. How do you think He felt about that? Have you ever felt more "special" away from home than at home? How could you help your family value you more?** (By valuing others in the family, for one thing.)

Have kids fill out the reproducible sheet, "Find Yourself." Let volunteers share and explain their answers, but don't press. Pay special attention to kids who seem to be searching or hurting, and talk with them later if possible. Encourage those who seem to be growing spiritually, too.

Find Yourself

Check all the boxes that apply to you.

In the Parable of the Sower, I'm like . . .

❑ The farmer, trying to tell others about Jesus

❑ The seed, letting God plant me wherever He chooses

❑ The sun, sometimes coming on too strong and "withering" people

❑ The birds, keeping people from hearing about Jesus

❑ The path, not able to believe because I've been stepped on too many times

❑ The rocky soil, too tough for God to get through to me

❑ The scorched plants, with a shallow foundation that can't keep me going

❑ The thorns, distracting Christians from all that religious stuff

❑ The choked plants, more interested in good times and money than in God

❑ The good soil, understanding and doing what God says

❑ The crop, glad that somebody told me about Jesus

In the Parable of the Weeds, I'm like . . .

❑ The enemy, keeping the youth group off balance because it's all a big joke anyway

❑ The servants, confused sometimes about what's good and what isn't

❑ The weeds, hoping nobody will notice that I'm not really a Christian

❑ The wheat, belonging to Christ

❑ The harvesters, ready to chop down evil

In the Parable of the Mustard Seed, I'm like. . .

❑ The man, willing to start with a little and believe that God will use it

❑ The mustard seed, with lots of potential for growth

❑ The tree, much more useful to God than I used to be

❑ The birds, glad that God cares for me as part of His kingdom

In the Parable of the Yeast, I'm like. . .

❑ The woman, ready to work hard with what God has given me

❑ The flour, under the influence of Christians but not one of them yet

❑ The yeast, making a difference for God in my part of the world

In the Parable of the Hidden Treasure, I'm like . . .

❑ The man, excited and joyful that I found Jesus

❑ The field, valuable because I belong to God

❑ The treasure, my real self hidden from most people

In the Parable of the Pearl, I'm like . . .

❑ The merchant, looking for the really important things in life

❑ The pearl, waiting for people to discover my value

In the Parable of the Net, I'm like . . .

❑ The fisherman, willing to do "dirty work" for God

❑ The net, reaching out to all kinds of people

❑ The "good" fish, looking forward to eternal life

❑ The "bad" fish, not sure what will happen to me when I die

Faith 101

The ministry of John the Baptist comes to a violent end after he boldly proclaims truth to some leaders who don't want to hear it. But Jesus and His disciples continue to minister, and Jesus astounds them with His miraculous power by feeding 5,000 and walking on water.

Cut the ten slips of paper from a copy of the reproducible sheet, "Can You Do It?" One at a time, have each person draw a slip and perform his or her activity. Later, explain that these were things your kids probably had never done before—but were capable of doing. So it is with following Jesus; we may find there is much we can do if we only give it a try.

DATE I USED THIS SESSION _____ GROUP I USED IT WITH _____

NOTES FOR NEXT TIME _____

_____

_____

1. Have you ever gotten in trouble for telling the truth? **What happened?** (Contrast these stories to the imprisonment and death of John the Baptist [vss. 1-12].)

2. So what if Herod married his brother's wife while the brother was still alive? It was against the law, but couldn't John have ignored it? (John's message was that the kingdom of God was at hand and that people should repent. Rulers needed to repent, too.)

3. Herod wanted to kill John, but didn't because of what the people would say. Then he was pressured into killing John because he'd made a foolish offer in front of his dinner guests. How have you allowed someone to embarrass you into doing something (good or bad) that you didn't want to do?

4. After John's death, Jesus withdrew to be by Himself. What do you suppose He may have been feeling and thinking? (Sadness over the death of a friend; knowing He would be killed eventually; importance of training His disciples to carry on, etc.)

5. It was impossible for Jesus to stay alone for long. A huge and hungry crowd awaited His return. Put yourself in place of one of the disciples when Jesus turned and said, "You give them something to eat" (vs. 16). What would you have done? (Compare to the disciples' lame excuse [vs. 17].)

6. What does this miracle (vss. 15-21) tell you about God's abilities, and your own? (He wants us to attempt bold, untried things for Him; sometimes we have enough [money, talent, etc.] to get something done for God, even when we don't think so; God has unexpected answers to our problems, etc.)

7. Do you ever think of Jesus as something other than the loving Son of God (a "ghost" [vs. 26], someone to be feared, a cruel judge, etc.)? If so, what do you do with those feelings?

8. Why do you think Peter challenged Jesus to invite him onto the water (vs. 28)? (Perhaps Peter wanted to believe more strongly in Jesus.) **What challenge would you like Jesus to help you meet?**

9. The wind and waves quickly overcame Peter's faith. What things tend to "pull you down" when you're trying to be faithful to God?

10. Why did Jesus scold Peter (vs. 31)? Peter was the only one who stepped out of the boat! (God's discipline is geared to our maturity. As we become more responsible as Christians, God expects more of us than when we were spiritual "babies.")

11. After seeing Jesus give power to a simple man like Peter, the disciples told Jesus, "Truly you are the Son of God." Have you ever seen God's power working in someone else? When? Has anyone ever seen God working through you? If so, when?

Designate one corner of the room as "A" and another as "B." Have kids stand between A and B to show which of the following statements they feel "closer" to. First, "When God has a big job for me, I (a) toss it right back to Him, or (b) dive in and do my best." Second, "When I need to take bigger risks with my faith (such as walking on water), I (a) cling to the mast with all my might, or (b) get out of the boat." Third, "When someone offends me, I (a) leave it in God's hands, or (b) get even as quickly as possible." Then brainstorm ways to increase personal levels of faith in Jesus.

Can You Do It?

GET DOWN ON ONE KNEE AND SERENADE SOMEONE IN THE ROOM

EXPLAIN (EVEN IF YOU HAVE TO MAKE IT UP) WHY A COMPASS NEEDLE ALWAYS POINTS NORTH

GIVE AN IMPROMPTU SPEECH ON "WHY I ADORE MY YOUTH LEADER"

PANTOMIME AN OCTOPUS MAKING A PEANUT BUTTER SANDWICH

IMITATE A MOUSE BEING EATEN BY A SNAKE

DRAW A PICTURE OF THE STATUE OF LIBERTY WHILE THE GROUP WATCHES

PLAY "JINGLE BELLS" ON AN IMAGINARY TUBA

PLAY AN "AIR GUITAR" VERSION OF "MARY HAD A LITTLE LAMB"

CALL OUT AT LEAST EIGHT WORDS THAT RHYME WITH "SPOON"

TAKE OFF YOUR SHOES AND JUGGLE THEM FOR 15 SECONDS

MATTHEW 15

Faith 201

Jesus has another confrontation with the Pharisees. Afterward He finds a Gentile woman with great faith, continues to heal the sick, and feeds 4,000 people with only seven loaves and a few small fish.

(Needed: Squirt gun and two blindfolds)

Form two teams. Each team chooses one volunteer to be blindfolded. Place a "loaded" squirt gun into an open area. Give the volunteers a spin, and at your signal their team members try to direct them (using only words) to the water pistol. The first to find it may remove his or her blindfold and put it to good use on the other person. This activity can lead into a discussion of "clean versus unclean" as well as "the blind leading the blind."

DATE I USED THIS SESSION _____ GROUP I USED IT WITH _____

NOTES FOR NEXT TIME_____

_____

_____

1. What are some things you've been criticized for this week? Was any of the criticism "nit-picky"?

2. The Pharisees accused Jesus' disciples of eating before washing their hands (vss. 1, 2). **According to the Pharisees, this would make them "unclean." How do you think the disciples felt about that?**

3. Jesus accused the Pharisees of stretching Scripture to suit their own purposes (vss. 3-6). **How do people do that today?** (They do what they want to do, then look for Scripture to back their actions; they quote certain portions and ignore others, etc.)

4. Faked worship (vss. 7-9) **is "in vain." Do you think it's better to go through the motions of worship than to give up worship completely? Explain.**

5. See verses 10-20. **What percentage of your "unclean" thoughts come out of your mouth? What percentage turn into unclean actions? What happens to the rest of them?**

6. Later, when Jesus was visited by the Canaanite woman (vss. 21-28), **He seemed to give her a hard time. Have you ever wanted something from God, but thought you might be bothering Him? What did you do?**

7. This lady wouldn't give up. She knew Jesus was a special Jewish leader (vs. 22) and that she wasn't Jewish. **But she asked a favor anyway. Why do you think she felt she had the right?** (Maybe she believed Jesus was powerful enough to provide for everyone—which, of course, He was.)

8. We now know that Jesus accepts any believer as a full-fledged member of His kingdom, with all the rights of an adopted child. **But if you didn't know this, would you be satisfied with the "crumbs" (vs. 27) He could provide? Why?** (The woman seemed to have such a clear grasp of Jesus' character that she knew the "crumbs" would be enough to provide anything she asked [vs. 28].)

9. The gathering of hungry crowds (vss. 29-39) was almost identical to one in Matthew 14. The disciples hadn't been able to handle the earlier incident, so why would Jesus call on them this time (vs. 32)? (He probably hoped they had learned something and would be ready to provide for the people. There were even more fish and loaves to work with this time. But the disciples were just as shortsighted as they had been previously.)

10. What are three things you think God wants you to do, but you're reluctant to do on your own? How could this group help you to do one of them?

11. Jesus' disciples depended a great deal on Him. If your parents and church leaders were to disappear today, do you think your spiritual life would get better or worse? Why?

The reproducible sheet, "Inside Story," will help group members think about attitudes they, like the Pharisees, may be covering up. Discuss the results: **If God knows everything, why try to hide your thoughts from Him? What would happen if we were 50% honest in this group? One hundred percent?**

Inside*Story*

What if our shadows showed what we were *really* thinking?

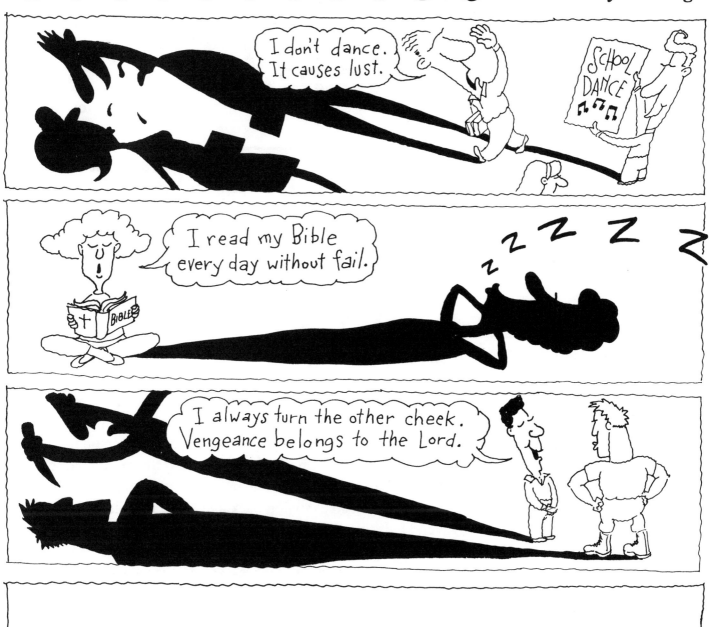

Now draw your own cartoon showing how your words sometimes don't match your actions. Choose from these captions if you like:

"He's from a cult, but I'm a true Christian." • "Don't you know that God wants you to take care of the environment?" • "Do unto others as you would have them do unto you." • "I would never smoke. It's sinful." • "I'll pray for you."

MATTHEW 16

Signs and Switchbacks

The conflict between Jesus and the Pharisees intensifies to the point where Jesus begins to prepare His disciples for His inevitable death. The disciples are beginning to catch on, but can't quite absorb everything they're seeing. After a bold profession by Peter, he soon proves that he does not yet understand everything.

(Needed: Noisemaker)

Explain that at your signal (bell, whistle, note on the piano, etc.), the person to your left must say as many good things about school as possible. At your next signal the person must switch to saying bad things about school. If the person pauses for more than three seconds, he or she is out. Signal often, causing the person to switch back and forth. Do this with several kids, working your way through the group. Change subjects (from school to cars to shampoo, etc.) if you like. Later, tie this in with Peter's back-and-forth statements about Jesus in Matthew 16.

DATE I USED THIS SESSION _____ GROUP I USED IT WITH _____

NOTES FOR NEXT TIME_____

_____

_____

1. Pass out the reproducible sheet, "Signs of the Times," and have kids follow the instructions. Many answers from the Isaiah passages are possible (birth of a son, one who bears others' sins, etc.) Concerning Matthew 1:4, ask: **What is the "sign of Jonah"?** (See Matthew 12:39-41, a reference to Jesus' burial and resurrection.)

2. **After all the miracles He'd performed, why wouldn't Jesus give the Pharisees the sign they asked for** (vss. 1-4)? (They'd already seen miracles; Jesus wasn't interested in putting on a show; He wanted people's faith in Him to continue even when He wasn't around to perform amazing signs, etc.)

3. **Do any of your friends want "signs" before they will believe in Jesus? How could you be a "sign" to them?**

4. **The disciples were confused when Jesus began to warn them about yeast** (vs. 6). **What are some groups today whose "yeast"** (vs. 12) **can be harmful?** (Any whose teaching isn't based completely on the Bible—Jehovah's Witnesses, New Agers, Mormons, etc.)

5. **Have you, like Peter** (vs. 16), **come to see who Jesus really is? If so, what led you to your conclusion?**

6. **If you could see Jesus standing in front of you, how might you express your faith to Him? How can you do that** *without* **seeing Him?**

7. **Jesus warned His disciples not to tell anyone that He was the Christ** (vs. 20). **Does that still apply to us? Why or why not?** (Jesus' time had not yet come to die. Later, however, He gave His followers specific instructions to tell the world what they had seen [Matthew 28:16-20].)

8. **If your best friend told you she and her family were moving to a very dangerous area to serve God, what would your reaction be? How is this like the events in verses 21-23?**

9. What have you "denied yourself" or given up in order to follow Jesus? Does verse 24 make you feel guilty, challenged, worried, or confused?

10. According to verse 26, even the whole world isn't worth losing your soul. Nobody gets the whole world, but what are some things people settle for as substitutes for the eternal life Jesus offers?

11. Based on the things you've done, what reward(s) do you expect from Jesus?

One minute Jesus was able to tell Peter, "Blessed are you," (Matthew 16:17), but not long afterward Jesus was saying, "Get behind me, Satan! You are a stumbling block to me" (Matthew 16:23). Many times we're like Peter—gaining stronger faith one minute and blocking God's will the next. Are you a blessing or a stumbling block in each of the following areas: Relationship with parents; dating habits; attitude toward chores; attention span in church; your innermost thoughts; life at school; the example you set for others; your party life; sports and extracurricular activities? Let kids share their responses if they want to. Then discuss: What would it take for you to convert your "stumbling blocks" into "stepping stones" to carry you (and others) closer to Jesus?

SiGNS OF THE TiMES

What "signs of the times" are described in the following passages? On the blank signposts, write or draw some of the things people are encouraged to look for in order to know that the Messiah has come. (See Isaiah 9:1-7; Isaiah 53; Matthew 16:1-4.)

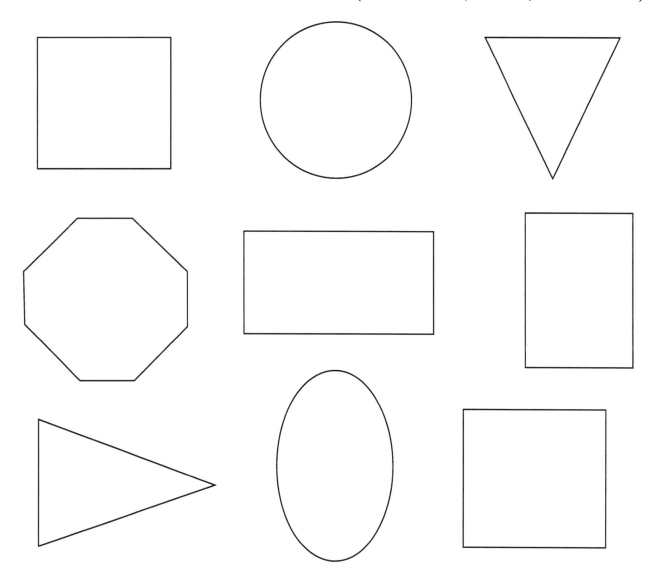

MATTHEW 17

Don't Hold The Mustard

Jesus takes aside three disciples to witness His transfiguration. Later, when the disciples can't perform a miracle, He teaches them about "mustard seed" faith. He also speaks openly about His death and shows Peter a unique way to pay his temple tax.

(Needed: Makeup, hair care products, etc.)

Ask volunteers to undergo "makeovers." Provide an assortment of grooming products, put kids in teams, and see which team can make the most improvement on its volunteer. (Use a Polaroid camera, if possible, to show before and after pictures.) Use this as a way to help explain what the term "transfiguration" (a change in form or appearance) means. Observe that the transfiguration in Matthew 17 is far more than a makeover, of course.

DATE I USED THIS SESSION _____ GROUP I USED IT WITH _____

NOTES FOR NEXT TIME _____

_____

_____

1. If you'd been one of the disciples, do you think Jesus would have singled you out to go see His transfiguration (vss. 1-9)? **Why?**

2. What do you think was the purpose of the transfiguration? (To show Christ's deity; to show that there is a different "glorified" body that God's people have after death—the "imperishable" body promised in I Corinthians 15:42-44.)

3. While witnessing this astounding event, the disciples heard God speak (vss. 5, 6). They were terrified. Have you ever thought that God wanted to tell you something? If so, how did it make you feel?

4. Jesus told the disciples not to be afraid (vss. 7-9) after He touched them. Why do you think He touched them? In what ways has Jesus "touched" or comforted you? How would you comfort a child, a friend, or an older person who was afraid?

5. Coming down from the mountain, Jesus explained that many people had missed out on the "Elijah" that God had sent to prepare the way for the Messiah (vss. 9-13). John the Baptist had come and gone, and never received the recognition he deserved. What people do you know who have served God without getting much attention? What do you think motivates them?

6. The disciples were a lot like us—Jesus had given them a job to do, and the authority to do it, yet they couldn't seem to get it right (vss. 14-18). Can you think of an example from the past week where a little more faith might have helped you through a tough challenge?

7. As a disciple, why might you have been so sad if Jesus told you He was going to die (vss. 22, 23)? (Loss of a friend; not receiving the "kingdom" you may have been expecting; not knowing what to do with your life since you had left everything to follow Him; fear of being associated with Him; etc.)

8. Are you ever sad about the suffering Jesus had to do? Or do you pretty much take His death for granted? Explain.

9. Of the people you know and love, whose death do you think would affect you most? Why? How long do you think it would take you to work through this person's death? (Don't get too morbid, but try to help students see that Jesus' prediction of His death had a real effect on the disciples.)

10. Why do you think Jesus didn't just take tax money out of the disciples' treasury rather than doing what He did (vss. 24-27)? (Perhaps He wanted to show that God could provide for needs in unexpected ways.)

11. Why was there just enough money for Jesus and Peter—not for everyone? (Perhaps because Peter was the one approached by the tax collectors, and may have been more concerned about the issue.)

The reproducible sheet, "Making Molehills Out of Mountains," can help group members connect their major problems with "mustard seeds" of faith. Give kids some time to work on these individually; then check to see if anyone needs assistance coming up with appropriate Scriptures to apply. Let kids discuss the results if they want to. (Answers to "explosives" matchups: 1[a]; 2[d]; 3[c]; 4[b].)

making molehills out of
MOUNTAINS

A mustard seed is about this big: •

Match the following mustard-seed-sized "explosives" with the effect they'd have on a mountain. (For a hint, see Matthew 17:20, 21.)

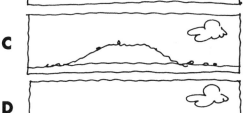
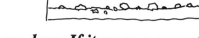

1. Gunpowder the size of a mustard seed   **A**

2. Faith the size of a mustard seed   **B**

3. Plutonium the size of a mustard seed   **C**

4. Dynamite the size of a mustard seed   **D**

Think about the biggest problem you're facing these days. If it were a mountain, how high would it be? (Circle one)

A	B	C	D

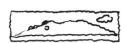

According to Jesus, how would faith the size of a mustard seed affect that mountain? (Circle one)

A	B	C	D

Which of the following verses, if you really believed them, could be like a mustard seed in blasting the biggest problem you're facing?

Exodus 4:11, 12   Psalm 121:1-3   Luke 12:22-24
Exodus 33:14   Proverbs 3:5, 6   Philippians 4:6, 7
Numbers 23:19   Isaiah 40:31   I Corinthians 10:13
Psalm 23:4   Jeremiah 29:11   Romans 8:31-39
Psalm 37:4, 5   Jeremiah 32:17   Revelation 7:16, 17

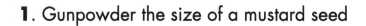

MATTHEW 18

Kid Stuff

Jesus uses a child to teach the disciples about the kingdom of heaven, parables to teach them about salvation and forgiveness, and common sense to help them learn more about handling conflict.

Open the session as if your young people were a primary class. Sing some simple songs ("Jesus Loves Me" or "The B-I-B-L-E"), tell a flannelgraph story, pull out the crayons and coloring books, or do a project using modeling clay. See how long you can go without getting too much resistance from the group. When you finally explain, lead into Jesus' call for us to be more like little children.

DATE I USED THIS SESSION _____ GROUP I USED IT WITH _____

NOTES FOR NEXT TIME _____

_____

_____

1. Do you have any little brothers or sisters? If so, have you ever considered that they might be "the greatest in the kingdom of heaven" (vss. 1-4)?

2. What do you think it was about little children that impressed Jesus so much? (Perhaps their openness, their trust in parents, etc.)

3. What's the difference between being child*ish* and being child*like*? ("Childish" usually refers to immaturity or other negative qualities of childhood. "Childlike" suggests innocence and wonder.)

4. What actions and attitudes do most teenagers in our society think are "grown-up"? (Drinking, driving, having sex, rebelling against authorities, having a job, etc.) **Which of these can get in the way of having a childlike attitude toward Christ?**

5. Think of your attitudes toward younger children. If you took Jesus' words literally (vss. 5-9), would you still have all your limbs? (Misleading anyone is a severe offense, but this is especially true when misleading children who trust those who are older. The seriousness of Jesus' command should cause us to increase our patience and "cut off" improper behavior or attitudes.)

6. Why do you think God has such a protective attitude toward children (vss. 10-14)? What are some dangers that children face today? (Child abuse and neglect, learning the wrong things from TV and other sources, gang violence, etc.) **What could your group do to help protect children in your area?**

7. What four rules for handling conflict can you find in verses 15-20? (A possibility: [1] No conflict situation should be left unresolved. [2] It's up to you to take the initiative. [3] If you can't work it out one-on-one, take an impartial referee with you. [4] If you still can't work it out, get your pastor or youth leader[s] involved. Then, even if the other person won't cooperate, you've at least done all you can do.)

8. If you've ever followed the preceding rules, what happened? When you *didn't* follow these rules, what happened?

9. Notice that this is a plan for when "your brother sins against you" (vs. 15). **Why do you think Jesus didn't say this was for when "you sin against your brother?"** (If someone is too stubborn to apologize to us, we're not excused from trying to work things out. Any conflict between people should be settled as quickly as possible. We can't sit back and smugly wait for the other person to come to us.)

10. Do verses 19 and 20 mean that if you get two other people to pray for a million dollars, you'll get it? Explain. (These verses are part of the instructions for dealing with conflict among Christians. They may refer to agreeing as a church on the verdict and the "sentence" in one of these conflict cases [vss. 16-18]. Other verses indicate that God will give us what we need, not necessarily what we want.)

Have kids follow the instructions on the reproducible sheet, "A Parable of You." Discuss the results. Then ask kids to act out, based on Matthew 18:21, 22, a new ending for the story.

A Parable of You

PARABLE CASTING

T hen _____ (your name) came to Jesus and asked, "Lord, how many times shall I forgive _____ (someone who bothers you) when he [or she] sins against me? Up to seven times?" Jesus answered, "I tell you, not seven times, but seventy-seven times.

"Therefore, the kingdom of heaven is like a king who wanted to settle accounts with his servants. As he began the settlement, _____ (your name), who owed him [forgiveness for]

_____

_____

(at least five things God has forgiven you for), was brought to him. Since [you were] not able to pay, the master ordered that _____ [you] and all that [you] had be sold to repay the debt.

"[You] fell on [your] knees before him. 'Be patient with me,' [you] begged, 'and I will pay back everything.' [Your] master took pity on [you], canceled the debt and let [you] go.

"But when [you] went out, [you] found one of [your] fellow servants who owed [you] _____ (something owed you by the person who bothers you). _____ [You] grabbed _____ (person who bothers you) and began to choke him [or her]. 'Pay back what you owe me!' _____ [you] demanded.

"[Your] fellow servant fell to his [or her] knees and begged [you], 'Be patient with me, and I will pay you back.'

"But [you] refused. Instead, [you] went off and _____ (the way you usually treat someone who really gets on your nerves). When the other servants saw what had happened, they were greatly distressed and went and told their master everything that had happened.

"Then the master called [you] in. 'You wicked servant,' he said, 'I canceled all that debt of yours because you begged me to. Shouldn't you have had mercy on your fellow servant just as I had on you?' In anger [your] master _____ (the way you usually treat someone who really gets on your nerves), until [you] should pay back all [you] owed.

"This is how my heavenly Father will treat each of you unless you forgive your brother from your heart." (Based on Matthew 18:21-35)

MATTHEW 19

Totally Tough Teachings

The Pharisees continue to test Jesus, this time about the matter of divorce. Jesus corrects some of their errors and emphasizes (again) the importance of childlikeness in regard to the kingdom of heaven. Later He talks with a rich young man who isn't quite willing to give up everything for the sake of the kingdom.

Plan an activity that requires a certain degree of physical flexibility and limberness (Twister, a limbo contest, an aerobics routine led by a double-jointed group member, etc.). After experiencing a certain degree of difficulty, the group should be able to better understand the "camel through the eye of the needle" concept that Jesus presents in this chapter.

DATE I USED THIS SESSION _____ GROUP I USED IT WITH _____

NOTES FOR NEXT TIME _____

_____

_____

1. If Jesus made His remarks about divorce on a TV talk show today (vss. 3-12), **how do you think the audience would react? From what you've seen of divorce, do you think following Jesus' teachings on the subject would make the world a better place or worse? Why?**

2. The Pharisees kept trying to trip Jesus up in a debate (vss. 1-3). **Has anyone ever argued with you about what you believe? What questions about God or the Bible might "trip you up,"and how would you deal with them?** (Some questioners, like the Pharisees, don't really want answers or help. For those who are sincere, you could offer to study the Bible with them to find out answers, or look in a book that provides answers, or ask a leader at church.)

3. The Pharisees had twisted Scripture, granting divorces to men for tiny mistakes by their wives—including accidentally burning dinner (vs. 7, and also see Deuteronomy 24:1-4). **What does Jesus' response** (vss. 4-8) **tell you about the importance of marriage?** (God takes marriage much more seriously than many of us do. It's intended to be a lifelong commitment.)

4. Do you agree with the response of the disciples in verse 10—that if marriage requires that much personal commitment, it's better to stay out of it? Why or why not?

5. If you get married someday, what do you hope it will be like? What ideas in this passage might help you stay married?

6. Eunuchs (vss. 11, 12) **were men who had been castrated, usually in order to oversee a woman or group of women without being a threat to another man. And according to Jesus, how else might someone become a "eunuch"?** (Without having an operation, some choose to remain unmarried [and abstain from sex] in order to devote their time and energy to work for God. Paul was one such person [see I Corinthians 7.])

7. Jesus had recently explained how important children were to God (Matthew 18: 1-14), **but the disciples hadn't**

caught on (vss. 13-15). **Which of Jesus' teachings are easiest for you to "forget" when the pressure's on?**

8. **What would you say if you were in a job interview and were asked, "Basically, are you a good person?"** (Answers should show that "good" is a vague term, needing a standard by which to be measured.)

9. **Do you think the young man** (vss. 16-22) **was "good"? Was he "good enough"?** (No matter how much goodness we display by our own efforts, eternal life comes from God alone. And until we're willing to put Him first, we must settle for less than the best.)

10. **Which of the rewards mentioned by Jesus** (vss. 28-30) **means the most to you? Why?**

11. **What have you "left behind"** (vs. 27) **to follow Jesus? What do you think He** *wants* **you to leave behind? In what ways are you "last"** (vs. 30)?

For the rich young ruler, the obstacle between himself and Jesus was money. The student sheet, "Obstacle Course," will help kids think of their own obstacles. Ask volunteers to complete aloud the sentence, "The one thing that most often comes between myself and a closer relationship with Jesus is _____." Spend some time in prayer, asking God for His help in overcoming the obstacles.

OBSTACLE COURSE

What gets in the way of your having a closer relationship with Jesus? Show on this "obstacle course" the things that tend to keep you away from Him. Write in the "height" of each obstacle to show how tough that one usually is for you to overcome.

START

FINISH LINE
(GOD'S KINGDOM)

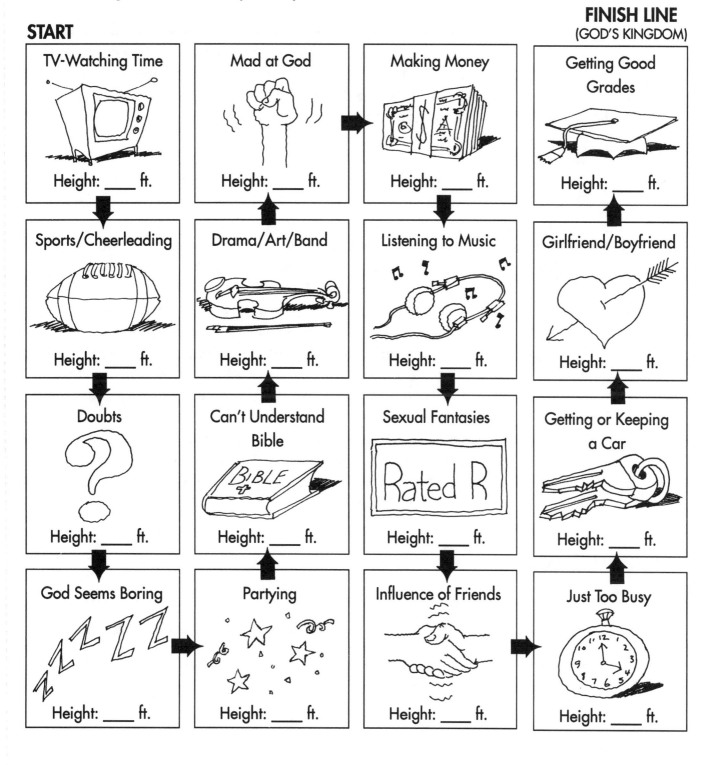

MATTHEW 20

Go to the End Of the Line

Jesus teaches about being first and last—by telling the Parable of the Workers in the Vineyard and by settling an argument among the disciples. He also predicts His death and gives sight to two blind men.

(Needed: A gift for each group member)

Think of an item that most of your group members would enjoy having, yet is affordable enough that you can provide one for each person (a favorite candy, the latest fad item, a dollar bill, etc.). Display two or three of the items prominently, but keep the rest hidden. As the group gathers, see who is willing to do the most to have one of what you're offering. Write and sign a "contract" (kids' offer in exchange for the item) with the highest bidders. If a few people just missed out on the bidding, pull out a couple more items and contract with those people as well. Finally, say something like: **I think I'll just give one to everybody—but I expect these contracts to be honored!** As protests arise, lead into the rest of the session.

DATE I USED THIS SESSION _____ GROUP I USED IT WITH _____

NOTES FOR NEXT TIME _____

_____

_____

1. If you'd been one of the first people to go to work for the landowner in the parable Jesus told (vss. 1-16), **how would you have felt at pay time? Why?**

2. Did the landowner do everything he said he would do? Did he cheat anyone? Was he completely fair? (That depends on your definition of "fair." The landowner was honest and followed through with everything he said he would do. He got complaints because he did *more* than he said he would do in some cases.) **What has God done for you that He didn't *have* to do?**

3. If the landowner represents God, what do you think this parable is supposed to teach? (Some possibilities: God would be letting Gentile believers into the kingdom of heaven, too, even though the Jews were "first" as His people; God doesn't want us to think in terms of "levels" of rewards, just that we are serving Him together; trusting God to provide for our needs is better than trying to "make a deal" with Him ["I'll do this if You do that."])

4. Look at verse 16. Can you name anyone who is "first" on earth who may be "last" in heaven? (Probably some celebrities, people in power, etc.) **Can you name anyone who is "last" here who may be "first" in heaven?** (People in your church who serve God faithfully without getting much credit; persecuted believers; believers who are looked down on because they're poor, disabled, etc.) **Where do you think you'll be in this "first and last" line? Why?**

5. If you'd been one of the disciples, how would you have reacted to Jesus' predictions about His death and resurrection (vss. 17-19)? **Why do you think the disciples' reaction wasn't recorded?**

6. Have you ever been embarrassed by a "helpful" parent or other relative (vss. 20-22)? What happened? What do you think the sons of Zebedee were thinking when their mother asked Jesus a favor?

7. How is the disciples' fight and Jesus' response (vss. 24-28) like the grumbling workers and the landowner's

response (vss. 9-16)? (The disciples and the workers were all trying to get what they felt they deserved; Jesus wanted them to quit demanding first place and be willing to serve Him.)

8. What "first place" award would you most like to get? Do you think God wants you to get it? When could competing for "number one" be good? Bad?

9. Act out your answers to the following. How might the events in verses 29-34 have been different if the blind men had given in to peer pressure? If they'd lost their nerve and asked for money instead of sight? If Jesus had been interested only in "important" people?

10. Does this chapter leave you feeling comforted, yelled at, worried, wanting to change, or something else? Why?

Ask kids to close their eyes, identifying with the blind men, as you read verses 29-34 again. Then let them open their eyes and individually fill out the student sheet, "Half and Half." Discuss their answers. Ask: **What can you learn from this chapter about receiving things from God?** (He's generous; He may surprise us; He doesn't always say yes; He can do anything, etc.)

HALF AND HALF

WE'VE WRITTEN THE FIRST HALVES OF SEVERAL SENTENCES BELOW. (WE DID THE HARD HALVES.) NOW IT'S UP TO YOU TO FINISH THEM UP. LENGTH DOESN'T MATTER; HONESTY DOES.

GIVE EACH QUESTION SOME THOUGHT, AND BE AS SPECIFIC AS YOU CAN.

I don't ask God for something unless . . . _____

When I want something from God, I usually . . . _____

If Jesus were to ask me right now, "What do you want me to do for you?" I would say . . . _____

The last time I asked God for something I didn't get, I . . . _____

If I had more faith, I would ask God for . . . _____

The people who knew Jesus in person were lucky because they . . . _____

Sometimes I don't bother asking God for stuff because . . . _____

In addition to the material *things* I need, I also wish God would . . . _____

Because of what God *has* done for me, I . . . _____

This week I'll ask God for . . . _____

MATTHEW 21

King for a Day

Jesus rides into Jerusalem, to the cheers of the people. While there, He drives the money changers out of the temple. Then He continues to heal the sick, answer the accusations of the Pharisees, perform miracles, and teach in parables.

Have each person act out one of the highlights of his or her life, using only nonverbal communication. Let others guess what's going on in each charade. Such events could include winning a big ball game, receiving an award, or going on a special vacation. Lead into the following questions by explaining that Palm Sunday was one of Jesus' "big" days—one of the few times when a large group of people seemed to recognize Him for who He really was.

DATE I USED THIS SESSION _____ GROUP I USED IT WITH _____

NOTES FOR NEXT TIME _____

_____

_____

1. Have you ever marched in a parade? If so, what was it like to be the "center of attention"?

2. How do you think Jesus felt as He entered Jerusalem (vss. 1-11) while everyone was cheering Him on? (He probably had mixed emotions. Maybe He was glad that people were finally beginning to offer praise, yet He knew it would be short-lived. He knew He would be crucified within the week.)

3. Can you name some celebrities who were popular a year or two ago, and now are "has-beens"? What happened? Have you ever gone from being "on top" to being a "nobody"? Have you ever been rejected by a friend? How did it feel?

4. In spite of Jesus' new popularity, He was willing to make people mad by defending God's temple (vss. 12-17). What have you done to get on the "good side" of the "right" people at school? How could obeying God get you on their "bad side"? Have you ever done the right thing even though it might mean losing friends? What happened?

5. When Jesus withered the fig tree, do you think He was really angry at a plant? What point was He making? (A leafy fig tree should have been fruitful, just as a "grown-up" or mature believer should be.)

6. If you really believed Jesus' promise in verses 21 and 22, what might you dare to ask for?

7. If verses 21 and 22 are true, why haven't you heard of any mountains being thrown into the sea? (Maybe because people don't have that much faith; maybe because our requests need to be in line with what God wants, and mountain-tossing hasn't been high on God's list of things to do.)

8. The Pharisees kept trying to get Jesus to say something that would get Him in trouble (vs. 23). But instead of losing control, He asked *them* a question *they* couldn't answer without getting into trouble. Can you come up with a situation in which you could do something like that instead of losing your temper?

9. Of the two sons Jesus describes in His parable (vss. 21-31), **which are you most like when it comes to your relationship with God? Why? What point do you think Jesus was making with this story?** (The Jewish people said they were looking for a Messiah, but most were going to reject Jesus. The Gentiles didn't know they were looking for a savior, but many of them were going to respond to Jesus and repent.)

10. **How do you think the tenants in the parable** (vss. 33-46) **would explain their actions in court if they were on trial for murder? How do you think those who executed Jesus would explain their actions? When people today reject Jesus, what reasons do they give?**

To wrap up your Q & A, hand out copies of "Interrogation," the reproducible student sheet. Ask students to complete them individually. Then discuss as a group—first taking a first-century view, then today's perspective.

Read and discuss this case study: **Kelly has been a Christian for three years. At first she thought Jesus was great, and welcomed Him into every part of her life. But things changed. When she prayed that her brother would be healed of leukemia, he died. When she tried to tell her friends about God, most of them rejected her. Now she feels angry at God. Today she read about the way people cheered for Jesus in Matthew 21. That reminded her of how she used to feel about Jesus. She wishes she could feel that way again, but doesn't want to fake it. What advice would you give Kelly?**

INTERROGATION

"Excuse me," the officer says to you. "I'm Centurion Spartacus Squadus of the Jerusalem Police Department. We're investigating several disturbances in the area today that we believe are connected to one person . . . a Mr. Jesus of Nazareth. I'd like to ask you a few questions. Just tell me what you saw."

(This guy looks serious. You'd better cooperate. Put yourself in the place of a first-century regular person, and answer the officer's questions based on what you believe to be true.)

"OK, the first charges we have are littering and causing a public disturbance. Was this Jesus person responsible for the cloaks and palm branches scattered throughout our public streets?"

"We also have reports that Mr. Jesus is a violent man—vandalizing tables at the temple and threatening business people. What can you tell me about his usual way of acting?"

"Some environmentalists are concerned about reports that Jesus has been destroying perfectly good fig trees. Is this a habit with him? If not, why would he do something like that?"

"Just a couple more questions and I'll let you go back to milking your goat. Can you give me any reason not to place this man under arrest right now? The Pharisees are ready to swear out a warrant."

"It seems some people are trying to pass Mr. Jesus off as the 'Son of God' or some such title. Based only on what you've seen of this man, who do you think he is?"

Come to the Party!

Jesus describes God's kingdom, using the Parable of the Wedding Banquet. As the Pharisees keep trying to make Him say something they can use against Him, Jesus answers their questions about taxes, marriage during the afterlife, and the greatest commandment. Then He asks them a question that shuts them up for good.

(Needed: One or more prizes)

Have a contest to see who's best at condensing story lines of well-known books or movies. Each plot must be "boiled down" to a sentence of 25 words or less. Try classics like *Moby Dick*, *The Wizard of Oz*, *Frankenstein*, and recent books or films. For added fun, have kids compete to see who can read their sentences fastest. Make the transition to Matthew 22 by having kids try to summarize the Bible in a single sentence. Later, compare their attempts to Jesus' statement in verses 37 and 38.

DATE I USED THIS SESSION _____ GROUP I USED IT WITH _____

NOTES FOR NEXT TIME _____

_____

_____

1. What's your idea of a perfect party? What's the best way to turn down an invitation to a party you *don't* want to attend?

2. Why didn't the people in the parable (vss. 1-14) go to the wedding party? (Some were too busy with other things, like their work. But all obviously didn't care enough about the king or his son to want to attend.)

3. If the king in the parable is God, who are the other characters? (Possibilities: The son is Christ; the servants are the prophets; the first and second invitees are God's chosen people, the Jews; the "the anyone you can find" invitees are the Gentiles; the man in the wrong clothes is one who lacks righteousness.)

4. How are you supposed to know whether you're "wearing the right clothes" to get into God's kingdom (vss. 8-14)? (Jesus provides the righteousness we need to enter the kingdom. If we turn from sin and put our trust in Him, our sins are forgiven; if we reject Him, He will reject us [vss. 11-13].)

5. The Pharisees were amazed by Jesus' answer about God and Caesar (vss. 15-22). Do you think His answer was amazing, confusing, a non-answer, or brilliant? What do you think He meant? (He probably meant that it was possible to pay required tribute to earthly governments *and* give God what He is due.)

6. How do kids today sometimes give to others what belongs to God? What belongs to God when it comes to your allowance or paycheck? Where your sexuality is concerned? Regarding your plans for career and/or college?

7. Next the Sadducees tried to trip Jesus up with a far-fetched "story problem" about life after death (vss. 23-33). How do you feel about His answer—that people in heaven, like the angels, won't marry?

8. What question would you like to ask Jesus about life after death? Why do you think He didn't spend more time on the subject? (It's natural to be curious about our futures, but Jesus came to give us a full, meaningful life *now* as well as later. There's a lot of work to be done for Him now, and maybe He didn't want to distract people from that.)

9. If the greatest commandment (vss. 34-40) sums up all the rest, why not throw out the rest of the Bible? (The rest of the Bible shows in more detail how to follow the greatest commandment. It also teaches us more than commands—it helps us understand God and what He's done, etc.)

10. Imagine being a president or king, but in disguise, and talking with regular people to see what they *truly* thought of you. What things would you want to find out?

11. Jesus was able to quiz people on what they thought of Him (vss. 41-45). Because He knew Scripture so well, He was able to stop the Pharisees from wasting His time with their traps. What kinds of traps waste your time, and how could knowing the Bible help you stay out of them?

Help kids think through what it means to follow the greatest commandment by having them work on the reproducible sheet, "With All Your Blanks." When they're done, discuss the results as kids are willing. If any ideas arise for using the items in group projects, follow through if possible.

WITH ALL YOUR BLANKS

"Love the Lord your God with all your _____ and with all your _____ and with all your _____."

Fill in the first blank with a word from column A, the second blank with a word from column B, and the third blank with a word from column C.

A	B	C
computer	hairstyle	diary
telephone	Saturdays	jokes
stomach	homework	CDs
mouth	dates	money
jewelry	keyboards	pets
car	drums	snacks
offering	muscles	hormones
eyes	study hall	dreams
fingers	desserts	spring vacation
shoes	sadness	prayers
lunch hours	friendships	games
anger	I.Q.	failures
parties	bedroom	subscriptions
camera	chores	job applications
lawn mower	Christmas	Sundays
video rentals	tests	presents

Now tell *specifically* how you could show your love for God by using each of the three things you chose.

I could show my love for God with item A by . . . _____

I could show my love for God with item B by . . . _____

I could show my love for God with item C by . . . _____

Now circle everything on the list that you think you're already loving God with.
Of the things left uncircled, choose one to work on this week.

MATTHEW 23

The Messiah Strikes Back

Having been hounded repeatedly by the Pharisees, Jesus comes out and says exactly what He thinks about them. He describes in bold detail their hypocrisy, their lack of love and failure to care about things that really matter, and His sense of loss for Jerusalem.

(Needed: Trash bags, filler, decorations, team prize)

Before the meeting, fill large trash bags with wadded-up newspaper or even smelly kitchen garbage. Tie them securely. At the meeting, have teams compete to see who can make their bags look the most glamorous in five minutes. Provide decorations (ribbon, cheap jewelry, tape, foil, neckties, etc.) for this purpose. After awarding a prize, talk about the idea of trying to look impressive on the outside when we're really rotten on the inside—the main charge Jesus leveled against the Pharisees.

DATE I USED THIS SESSION _____ GROUP I USED IT WITH _____

NOTES FOR NEXT TIME _____

_____

_____

1. Who's the last person you really told off? What was the occasion? Looking back, was it a good or bad idea?

2. We don't often think of Jesus calling people names and verbally expressing His anger, but He does in Matthew 23. Why do you think He comes down so hard on the Pharisees? (They were "using" religion for their own purposes, and abusing the truths people trusted them to keep. And they didn't just disagree with Jesus; they worked to make Him look bad. That meant they were rejecting all the truth He was sharing with them.)

3. Do you learn more about God by what people tell you, or by seeing the way they live? Give examples.

4. Everything the Pharisees did was for "show" (see vss. 5-7). What kinds of clothes and ways of talking are seen as "spiritual" today? In this group?

5. Does Jesus mean that you shouldn't call your dad "Father" (vss. 8-12)? (No. His point is that sometimes people try to get recognition for something God deserves credit for.)

6. Jesus describes a scene where the Pharisees are sort of gathered in the doorway of the kingdom of heaven, not wanting to go in, and trying not to allow anyone else in, either (vss. 13-15). How could a Christian kid today "block the doorway" for others who might want to come into the kingdom? Where do you "stand" at the door-way—blocking people or ushering them in?

7. Some Pharisees would actually strain their drinking water to keep from accidentally consuming a gnat (an unclean animal)! Yet Jesus charged that they would "swallow a camel" (vs. 23). What are some of the "gnats" and "camels" that you've seen among Christians?

8. The Pharisees hid their rotten attitudes with impressive words and appearances (vss. 25-28). What would your school be like if everyone's real selves "leaked through" and could be seen? What would our group be like if we could read each other's thoughts during a meeting? What kinds of thoughts might we want to hide from each other?

9. In spite of everything they were doing wrong, how did Jesus feel about the people of Jerusalem (vss. 37-39)? (He was loving and sad, but He would not force people to accept Him.)

10. How do you think Jesus feels when you do something wrong? (Probably much the same way.)

11. Jesus really lets the Pharisees have it in this chapter. Does that mean we should do the same to people when we're mad? Why or why not? (Not usually. Note that Jesus lashed out at the way the Pharisees sinned and caused others to sin, not at their criticism of Him. He was also sinless, and as the Son of God was qualified to judge others. We should stand against evil, and it's OK to be angry, but "Man's anger does not bring about the righteous life that God desires" [James 1:20].)

Have three kids act out the skit on the reproducible sheet, "Pharisees: The Next Generation." Let other kids provide the explosive sound effects. Then discuss how the Captain failed to see the "big picture" because he, like the Pharisees, was too concerned with the little things. Ask kids which item in each of the following pairs they tend to pay more attention to, and why: (1) praying in a certain way before meals versus feeding victims of famine; (2) making the right impression in front of church friends versus telling non-Christian friends about Jesus; and (3) not being caught reading a porno magazine versus not thinking lustfully about the opposite sex. **Are all of these important? How can you remember the "big picture" this week?**

PHARISEES: THE NEXT GENERATION

Cast: Captain Nitpicker, Commander Detail, Lieutenant Gorf

Time: The future

Place: The starship *Trivialize*

NITPICKER: Steady as she goes, Commander Detail. What is our current speed?

DETAIL: Approximately Warp 5, captain.

NITPICKER: I need our *exact* speed, Commander.

DETAIL: Exactly Warp 5.1003402, Captain.

NITPICKER: I mean our exact *exact* speed.

DETAIL: Computed to the thirty-ninth decimal place, our precise speed would be—

GORF: Excuse me, Captain. There is an unidentified craft off the starboard bow.

NITPICKER: What color is it?

GORF: Color? Uh—sort of a grayish-green, Captain.

NITPICKER: Is it a *dark* grayish-green, or a *light* grayish-green?

GORF: Uh, sort of dark. With red lights on the—

NITPICKER: How many red lights?

GORF: Let me see. . . . One, two, three . . .

(There is a huge explosion. The crew is rocked back and forth.)

GORF: Captain! The unidentified vessel is firing on us!

NITPICKER: That's not important. How many red lights does it have?

DETAIL: I believe there are 74 red lights, Captain, not including two amber lights on the vessel's tail.

NITPICKER: Very good, Detail. I can always count on you to tell me the important things.

(There is a another explosion. The crew is knocked to the floor.)

GORF: Captain! We have damage to the outer hull! We will self-destruct in approximately 19 seconds!

NITPICKER: *Exactly* how many seconds?

GORF: Uh, 16.3. No, now it's 11.5. No, now it's 8.1. No, now it's . . .

NITPICKER: Never mind. At a time like this, we must concentrate on the truly important things! Exactly *how* dark grayish-green is that—

(There is a gigantic explosion. The crew is dead, except for NITPICKER, who can barely crawl to push a button on his chair.)

NITPICKER: Uhh . . . Captain's final log . . . stardate 4994.67 . . . Or is that 4994.68? I— *(He falls to the floor, dead.)*

The End

Your Time Is Almost Up

Jesus has begun to talk about His forthcoming death, and the disciples have a number of questions. Jesus sits down with them to discuss the signs of His coming, to warn them of things to watch out for, and to encourage them to remain faithful.

(Needed: Stopwatch or watch with a second hand; small prize)

Have group members stand. Designate a length of time for them to estimate (30 seconds, a minute, etc.). They should sit down when they think that length of time has passed. The person who is closest to the correct time wins a small prize. Make it tougher by distracting kids to keep them from counting the seconds—ask them questions, have them sing, or do exercises as a group. After the contest, tie it in to the Matthew 24 theme of waiting and wanting to know the specific time of Jesus' return.

DATE I USED THIS SESSION _____ GROUP I USED IT WITH _____

NOTES FOR NEXT TIME _____

_____

_____

1. About how old were you when you first thought about how the world might end? What did you think? How did it make you feel?

2. The disciples came to Jesus "privately" (vs. 3) to find out what He knew about the end of things. How does His warning to the disciples (vss. 4, 5) also apply to you? (There are always people who claim to speak for Jesus but really don't—as well as those who claim to know when He will return. We need to be careful who we believe.)

3. How have you seen the end of the world, or Jesus' return, portrayed in movies and books? (Many have involved nuclear holocaust or some kind of "antichrist" child who doesn't quite match biblical prophecies.) How do these compare to the events described by Jesus in verses 4-22?

4. In addition to visible signs, what spiritual dangers will be present (vss. 23-28)? (Some will pose as Jesus, with power to perform miracles.)

5. How can people then (and now) keep from being fooled by a "Jesus impersonator"? (Some of the fakes will be good enough to fool a lot of people [vs. 24]. But just as lightning in the sky is unmistakable, so will be the coming of the real Jesus [vs. 27]. Those who get to know Jesus well *now* will know Him *then*.)

6. Which event in this chapter is scariest to you? Why? Which would you most like to see? Why?

7. Why will people mourn (vs. 30)? (It will be too late for anyone who hasn't chosen to follow Christ.) What do you think nonbelievers will think of their Christian friends then?

8. Some people say they've figured out exactly when all these things are going to happen. How specific did Jesus get (vss. 32-36)? (When all the signs listed begin to take place, people can expect Jesus to return soon—but not even Jesus knew the exact time.)

9. Why do you think God is so secretive about when all this is going to happen? (Maybe if He gave us the exact date, most of us would live our own way until the last minute and then try to "get religion." Maybe we wouldn't bother to spread the news about Jesus if we thought there wasn't time—or we knew the date was far into the future.)

10. Look at verses 42-51. How would you paraphrase them for someone who didn't understand the words "watch," "thief," "faithful," "servant," and "master"?

11. What three words would you use to describe your own feelings about the return of Jesus and the end of the world?

Wrap up your Q & A by having kids fill in the reproducible sheet, "Last Days Checklist." Discuss, keeping in mind that scholars' opinions vary on these issues. If questions arise that you can't answer, ask volunteers to research (using commentaries and books on prophecy) and report at the next meeting.

Assign individuals or teams to represent the following: (1) A scientist who says the world won't end for millions of years, and by then humans will live in other solar systems; (2) a self-appointed prophet who says Jesus will return a week from next Tuesday; (3) an activist who says pollution or nuclear holocaust will destroy the human race within 50 years; (4) a Christian who believes Jesus will return soon, but doesn't know whether "soon" means an hour or a thousand years. Have each person or team write a "to do" list for the next week, based on that character's beliefs. Then share and discuss results. If time allows, have kids write personal "to do" lists with Jesus' return in mind.

LAST *Days*
C H E C K L I S T

Jesus listed things that will happen during the "last days" before His return to earth. Which of these things have already taken place? Which are happening now? Which are still in the future? Make a check mark in the appropriate column to show what you think.

	Has already happened	Is taking place now, but isn't a "last days" sign	Is taking place now, and may be a "last days" sign	Is still in the future
Not one stone in Jerusalem will be left on another				
Many will come claiming, "I am the Christ"				
Wars and rumors of wars				
Famines				
Earthquakes				
Christians persecuted, hated, and put to death				
Many will turn away from the faith and betray and hate each other				
False prophets will appear and deceive many				
Wickedness will increase and love will grow cold				
The Gospel of the kingdom will be preached in the whole world				
The sun and moon will be darkened				

MATTHEW 25

What to Do until Jesus Comes

Jesus tells three parables to help the disciples understand and prepare for His eventual second coming: the parable of the ten virgins, the parable of the talents, and the parable of the sheep and goats.

(Needed: Team prize)

Before the session, cut the questions from a copy of the reproducible sheet, "Sheep and Goats." Put the "Sheep" and "Goat" questions in separate stacks. When the meeting starts, have kids line up single-file. Don't tell them beforehand that one stack of questions is tougher than the other. The first student must choose from the "Sheep" stack, the second from the "Goat" stack, etc. Kids who answer correctly enter the "Sheep" group (on the right) and get a prize. Those who don't are "Goats" (on the left) and must perform a task of your choice. Act as if nothing is amiss until kids begin to complain. Ask them to describe their feelings later as you discuss the parable of the sheep and the goats.

DATE I USED THIS SESSION _____ GROUP I USED IT WITH _____

NOTES FOR NEXT TIME _____

_____

_____

1. Have you ever taken part in a wedding? If so, what was it like? If not, what do you think it would be like to be a best man or a bridesmaid?

2. How would you feel if you were attending a wedding where half the bridesmaids didn't show up? (Sadness for the bride and groom; embarrassment; maybe anger.)

3. In Jesus' story (vss. 1-13), the foolish bridesmaids (virgins) were caught off guard because the bridegroom was late. What do you think of that excuse? (Pretty flimsy—the other five were prepared.)

4. Were the five prepared ones selfish because they didn't share (vss. 8, 9)? What would you have done in their place? (Point out that entering the kingdom of God requires an individual decision. Oil can be shared, but personal faith isn't transferable. No one can "prepare" for someone else.)

5. In the second parable (vss. 14-30), a *talent* is a unit of money (over $1,000). Our word *talent* (a skill) comes from this story. On a scale of 1 to 5, how many "money" talents do you think God has given you? How many "skill" talents?

6. Think of your abilities. Which have you put to work for God's benefit (vs. 16)? How? Which have you used only for yourself? How? Which have you hidden or not used at all (vs. 18)? Why?

7. Keeping the end of the "talent" story in mind, do you think God is exactly like the master? Why or why not? (Encourage kids to describe honestly their views of God. Note that the master seems harsher than the image most of us have of God, and God isn't money-hungry. Yet He is very serious about accomplishing His goals through us, and punishes laziness and wickedness [vs. 26].)

8. The third parable (vss. 31-46) describes two groups who get a big surprise. The "sheep" weren't expecting rewards for treating "little" people with kindness; the "goats" thought they could be "religious" enough while ignoring the needs of others. If someone had watched your every move last week, which group would they think you're in? What chances to be a "sheep" last week did you take? Which did you ignore?

9. All three parables in this chapter end with people being shut out, thrown out, and sent out to be punished. How do you feel about that? Why can't we just rewrite the endings so they're happy? (Jesus was stressing the importance of obeying Him until He returns. We may not like the idea of hell and punishment, but Jesus made it clear here and elsewhere that hell is real.)

10. If I gave you $10, what's the best thing you could do with it to help hungry or thirsty people? Those who don't have homes or enough clothes? Prisoners? What will you actually do with the next $10 you get?

As a group, brainstorm a "top ten" list—the ten most important things your whole group should try to accomplish before Jesus returns. Then assign these goals to small groups, who are to come up with specific ways to accomplish the goals. Share the results. Before the meeting ends, try to take at least one of the steps from the small group lists. If possible, follow through on the goals in weeks to come.

SHEEP&GOATS

SHEEP QUESTIONS

1. What age do you have to be to see a "G" movie?

2. Who's buried in Grant's tomb?

3. Who was created first, Adam or Eve?

4. Which is heavier, iron or feathers?

5. Which is longer, Genesis or I John?

6. Who is the current president of the United States?

7. What is the speed limit in a 55 m.p.h. zone?

8. What is the last book of the Bible?

9. What giant did David kill?

10. How many nostrils do you have?

11. Was the apostle Paul imprisoned in Rome or Detroit?

12. What whole number comes after 16?

GOAT QUESTIONS

1. How tall is the Eiffel Tower?

2. What Hebrew word means both "house" and "two"?

3. Who was the 13th U.S. President?

4. What metals do the letters "Au," "Hg," and "Pb" stand for?

5. How far was the village of Emmaus from Jerusalem?

6. According to Leviticus 24:11, who was the father of Shelomith?

7. Who played Jethro in the TV show, *The Beverly Hillbillies*?

8. How many milliliters equal 12 fluid ounces?

9. What Old Testament book tells the story of Mordecai?

10. What was the name of Rocky's girlfriend in the movie *Rocky*?

11. How many bowls are poured out in Revelation 16?

12. What was the family's favorite cartoon show on *The Simpsons*?

Answers to goat questions:
1. 984 feet (300 meters) 2. Beth 3. Millard Fillmore 4. Gold, mercury, and lead 5. Seven miles 6. Dibri 7. Max Baer, Jr. 8. 355 9. Esther 10. Adrian 11. Seven 12. The Itchy and Scratchy Show.

MATTHEW 26

Dinner and Desertion

As Jesus gets nearer His crucifixion, He undergoes a sequence of trials. Though He receives adulation from one woman in Bethany, the Pharisees continue to plot against Him; Judas betrays Him; He has His Last Supper, spends time in Gethsemane, is arrested by the chief priests, and is deserted and denied by His disciples.

(Needed: Refreshments)

Stage a brief "going away" party, complete with food, for a member of your group or an adult in your church. The catch is that the guest of honor is "going away" to death row, to be executed for a crime he or she didn't commit. After a few minutes of "festivities," discuss the mixed feelings and awkwardness of this "last supper." How might it compare to the last meal Jesus shared with His disciples?

DATE I USED THIS SESSION _____ GROUP I USED IT WITH _____

NOTES FOR NEXT TIME _____

_____

_____

1. What happened the last time someone seriously disappointed you, let you down, or hurt your feelings?

2. Any kind of emotional letdown hurts, but how do you feel if you discover someone has been scheming against you (vss. 3-5, 14-16)?

3. When the perfume was poured on Jesus' head (vss. 6-13), would you have agreed with the disciples that it was a waste of money that should have been put to better use? Or would you have thought the woman's action was right? (She saw something very special in Jesus. Since He was about to die, her action was especially appreciated; He defended what she did. Contrast this to the way Judas got money to betray Jesus [vss. 14-16].)

4. After spending about three years with Jesus and seeing His power, do you think Judas really thought he could fool Jesus (vss. 20-25)? If not, why do you think he tried? (Maybe Judas didn't care; maybe he wanted special attention; maybe he wanted to push Jesus into being a political or military Messiah.)

5. After explaining the symbolism of the bread and wine (vss. 26-30) and the forgiveness of sin He would provide, Jesus warned that He would be arrested and the disciples would desert Him. Right away they made a promise they couldn't keep (vss. 31-35). Do you think they meant it? If so, why didn't they follow through? What kinds of promises do kids make to God that they don't keep?

6. Jesus asked for prayer support from Peter, James, and John (vss. 36-46). They let Him down three times. Yet Peter didn't hesitate to draw a sword and try to fight (vss. 47-54). Do you think most people would rather solve problems by "really doing something" instead of "just praying"? Why? How do *you* solve problems?

7. Why do you think Peter followed behind Jesus (vs. 58)? Why do you think he denied Jesus so strongly (vss. 69-75)? (Maybe Peter was caught in the middle—between wanting total commitment and fearing the consequences—as many kids are.)

8. How do you think Jesus felt as He was supposed to defend Himself in front of people who couldn't possibly understand Him? If you feel misunderstood by non-Christian kids, what do you do?

9. Of everything Jesus went through during this time of His life, what do you think was the worst? Why? (Students' answers may hint at the things they fear most about expressing their faith.)

10. As Christians take "the Lord's Supper" today, they remember how Jesus gave His body and blood for the forgiveness of sins. If you were going to invent a group activity to help people remember what Jesus suffered in this chapter, what would it be?

Jesus knew ahead of time that He was going to be betrayed, deserted, humiliated, and killed. He could have chickened out, fought, or just worried. But He spent time praying, preparing for what was to come. Hand out copies of the reproducible sheet, "Prayer Check," to help kids evaluate their own prayer habits. Discuss the results as kids are willing. Consider a group prayer project (keeping journals, conducting a 30-day challenge, holding each other accountable, etc.). Also consider playing the Petra song, "Judas Kiss." It's a hard-edged yet thought-provoking song that parallels Judas's betrayal of Jesus with the sins we commit today.

1. The first three words that come to mind when I think of prayer are:

_____   _____   _____

2. To be honest, my approach to prayer is:

_____ I think it's important, and I pray when I get around to it

_____ I say some kind of prayer almost every day, whether or not I think about what I'm saying

_____ We pray so much at church that I really don't see much need for it on my own

_____ I talk to God on the spur of the moment. Some days I pray a lot and some just a little. But I think we're on pretty good terms

_____ Other:

3. My typical prayer contains:

_____ % praise, just for who God is

_____ % thanksgiving, for the things God has done for me

_____ % confession, telling Him what I've done wrong and asking forgiveness

_____ % petition, asking Him for things I want and need

_____ % intercession, requesting help for the needs of other people

_____ % other

4. How likely would you be to pray in each of the following situations?

	Very Likely	Somewhat Likely	I Can't Be Sure	I'd Probably Forget
• A friend is in a serious car wreck				
• I get straight A's for the first time				
• My parents aren't getting along				
• I *really* want a car				
• I face a final I haven't studied for				
• I'm free on a really great Saturday				
• Church is canceled due to bad weather				
• A relative is having serious surgery				
• I steal something and feel guilty				
• If I don't get $50 by Friday, I can't go skiing with the youth group				

5. If God chose three words to describe my prayer life, He'd probably say it is:

_____   _____   _____

An Innocent Man

The time has come for Jesus' arrest and crucifixion. He is taken before Pilate, rejected by the people, and sentenced. Then He is mocked, crucified, and buried in a tomb. The Pharisees place a guard at the tomb to make sure nothing happens to the body.

If possible, have kids sit in a circle. Go around the circle, giving each person ten seconds or less to answer a question about where he or she was when a well-known event occurred. For instance: **Where were you when the Persian Gulf War started? When President Bush got sick on a trip to Japan? When the movie *Hook* opened? When the midweek Bible study started last week? When the *Challenger* space shuttle exploded? When the Soviet Union went out of business?** Keep kids' ages in mind as you make up questions. Use the same question more than once if you wish, but use enough questions that kids won't know which to expect. Anyone who can't answer in time is out. After the game, discuss the big events kids remember best. Ask: **If you'd been alive when Jesus was crucified, where do you think you would have been? If you'd been there, what would you have remembered from the event?**

DATE I USED THIS SESSION _____ GROUP I USED IT WITH _____

NOTES FOR NEXT TIME_____

_____

_____

1. Let's divide Matthew 27 into seven "scenes" (vss. 1-10; 11-26; 27-31; 32-44; 45-56; 57-61; 62-66). You're going to film one of these scenes. What kind of music would you use in the background? Why?

2. Judas couldn't live with himself (vss. 1-10). Other than suicide, what are some things kids do because they feel extremely guilty?

3. Do you think Jesus would have forgiven Judas? If not, why not? If so, why are we sometimes so hard on ourselves when we sin? (Jesus later forgave all the disciples for deserting Him; surely He would have forgiven Judas had he asked. Like Judas, we lose God's perspective. We need to really believe in the power of forgiveness, because our own situations can look just as hopeless.)

4. What do you think of Pilate's attitude toward Jesus (vss. 11-26)? Do you know anyone like Pilate? (Many people today may be impressed with Christian values, yet make no personal commitment to Christ.)

5. If you had been Barabbas (vss. 15-26), how would you have felt? (Shocked, relieved, etc. In a way, Barabbas represents each of us—because Jesus died in our place.)

6. How do you feel when you read about Jesus' treatment by the mocking soldiers (vss. 27-31)? How do people mock Him today? (Some actually ridicule Jesus; but in a way, we mock Jesus' sacrificial death whenever we knowingly disobey Him.)

7. The crucified robbers and people watching also mocked Him (vss. 32-44) because they assumed that if He had power, He could escape. He chose not to use that power. How might obeying God mean not using your "power" in a basketball game? On a school bus? With a girlfriend or boyfriend? In a conversation with a parent?

8. How do you feel when it seems God is far from you? Do you express yourself honestly, as Jesus did (vss. 45, 46)?

9. If you'd never believed in Jesus before, do you think you might have changed your mind at His crucifixion (vss. 47-56)? Why? (The torn temple curtain, earthquake, and walking dead may have changed some people's opinions.)

10. Even the Pharisees remembered that Jesus had promised to rise from the dead after three days (vss. 62-64). Why didn't the disciples seem to recall this? (They were in shock; they didn't believe it; they hadn't understood, etc.) How would you have spent the next two days if you'd been a disciple?

11. If you'd been a Pharisee (vss. 62-66), how would you have felt after Jesus' death? Guilty? Satisfied? Worried? Why?

People had varying responses to Jesus' life and death. Let students use the reproducible sheet, "Snapshots," to compare themselves with some of the characters from Matthew 27. Discuss their answers and ask which characters kids want to be more like.

SNAPSHOTs

Which of the following people are you like? How?

Judas Iscariot (vss. 1-10)—Was a close friend of Jesus, yet sold Him out for a quick profit. The guilt of his betrayal plagued him until he killed himself.

Pilate (vss. 11-26)—Seemed to respect Jesus, but wanting to be popular kept him from acting on any feelings he may have had. He tried to trade Barabbas for Jesus, and he washed his hands, but we don't know that he made any kind of profession of belief in Jesus.

The mocking soldiers (vss. 27-31)—Everything they did ridiculed Jesus—clothing Him in a robe and crown of thorns, mocking Him, pretending to worship, spitting on Him, striking Him in the head again and again . . . and crucifying Him.

Mrs. Pilate (vs. 19)—Proclaimed Jesus' innocence from a distance and didn't want anything to happen to Him. Yet her action wasn't based on a personal relationship with Him.

The centurion (vs. 54)—Though probably not a follower of Jesus before, he saw enough evidence during the crucifixion to say that Jesus must surely have been the Son of God.

Simon of Cyrene (vs. 32)—He served Jesus because someone else forced him to. Did he keep serving? We don't know.

Barabbas (vss. 15-26)—He was guilty, but was set free because Jesus died in his place. Did this make a difference in his life? We don't know.

The faithful women (vss. 55, 56)—Mary Magdalene, Mary (the mother of Jesus), still another Mary, and other women had faithfully supported Jesus throughout His life. They continued to do so even in His death.

The thieves on the crosses (vss. 38-40)—They rejected God in life *and* in death (though we learn from Luke [23:39-43] that one of them eventually repented.)

Joseph of Arimathea (vss. 57-60)—Though a rich man and important official, Joseph took a stand for Jesus, taking this risk even after Jesus' death when it would have gained him nothing.

The Pharisees (vss. 1, 2, 41-43, 62-66)—What a bunch of phonies! While they did whatever they could to *look* religious, their motives were evil.

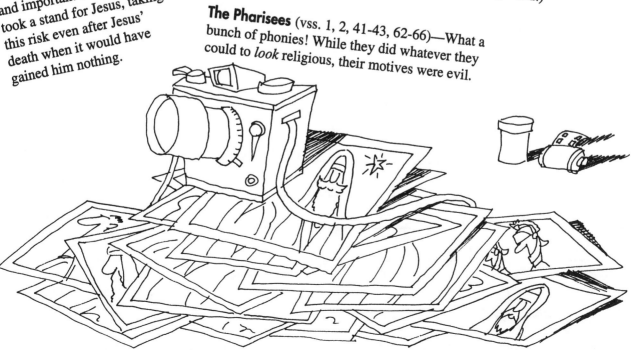

MATTHEW 28

The World's Greatest Comeback

As the women go to Jesus' tomb, they witness an earthquake and an angel who tells them Jesus has risen. Later, Jesus Himself appears and encourages them. As the Pharisees try to cover the truth of the resurrection, Jesus gives His people final instructions on how to carry on.

(Needed: Team prize)

Form teams. Each team's job will be to do something that surprises the other teams. The team that comes up with the biggest surprise wins a prize. Some ideas for surprises: Suddenly breaking into song; not trying at all to win the contest; giving money to another team, etc. After the contest, talk about the surprise of Jesus' resurrection. Jesus had clearly predicted it, yet His friends and enemies alike were surprised when it actually happened.

DATE I USED THIS SESSION _____ GROUP I USED IT WITH _____

NOTES FOR NEXT TIME _____

_____

_____

1. Suppose Abraham Lincoln, John F. Kennedy, and Elvis Presley walked in right now—in the flesh. What reactions do you think we would have? (Fear, disbelief, fascination, etc. Jesus' resurrection evoked similar emotions.)

2. The women (vs. 1) were on the way to the tomb to put burial spices on Jesus' body (Luke 24:1). The male disciples apparently were hiding out. Who does most of the work in your group, guys or girls? Who gets most of the credit? How can you make sure that everyone's contribution is valued?

3. How do you think the women were going to roll that heavy stone (vs. 2) away from the entrance of the tomb? (Maybe they didn't know about it, or thought someone would help them. Maybe they had a great deal of faith that it would be taken care of. Whatever they thought, they didn't let worrying about the stone keep them from trying to honor Jesus.)

4. Seeing an angel would surprise any of us. The Roman soldiers "shook and became like dead men" (vs. 4). The women were scared, too (vs. 8), but how was their reaction different? (Though frightened, the women were also filled with joy.) When you think of God, do you feel more fear or joy? Why?

5. The angel's advice (vss. 5-7) was good: (1) Witness this great event, (2) get the facts straight, and (3) tell others. How can you do the same thing? (Be sure of what you believe; be able to give personal examples of answered prayer, etc. Stay in control [not afraid] and be obedient.)

6. How might this account of Jesus' resurrection be different if video cameras and telephones had existed then? If you had seen Jesus alive that morning, what would you have done with a video camera and a telephone?

7. The Pharisees tried a cover-up (vss. 11-15). They wanted to convince everyone that Jesus' disciples, who had run like jackrabbits at His arrest, had sneaked past highly trained Roman guards and taken the body away.

Would you have believed this story or not? (Roman soldiers could be killed for sleeping on the job; this wasn't in the nature of the disciples; all but one of the disciples later died for Jesus, which could have been avoided if they had only produced the body; etc.)

8. When Jesus reappeared to His disciples, "they worshiped Him; but some doubted" (vs. 17). **Do you ever doubt while you worship, or worship while you doubt? Is that OK? Explain.**

9. Verses 18-20 contain the "famous last words" of Jesus. **How are people today still doing what He commanded?** (As pastors, missionaries, Christian musicians, "average" believers who tell others about Jesus, etc.)

10. How are *you* **doing what He commanded?**

11. If the last thing you'd done before Jesus' death was to desert Him, how would you feel to see Him alive again? (Ashamed; forgiven; determined to do better from now on, etc.)

12. If you'd been one of the disciples, and Jesus had said, "OK, I'll answer one last question before I go," what question would you have wanted to ask? How would His last sentence (in vs. 20) leave you feeling? How do you, today, feel about it?

Hand out copies of "Famous Last Words," the reproducible sheet. Help kids break down "The Great Commission" into an assignment they can relate to. After kids do some drawing, discuss. Then ask: **What motivated the original disciples to follow these instructions from Jesus? What would motivate you?**

There's a wrong way and a right way to do most things. What's the right way for *you* to follow through on the "famous last words" of Jesus? We've supplied some wrong ways. You draw some right ways in the boxes, OK?

G O

Wrong Way   Right Way

MAKE DISCIPLES

Wrong Way   Right Way

BAPTIZE THEM IN THE NAME OF THE FATHER AND OF THE SON AND OF THE HOLY SPIRIT
(or help them "go public" with their faith in Jesus)

Wrong Way   Right Way

TEACH THEM TO OBEY EVERYTHING I HAVE COMMANDED YOU

Wrong Way   Right Way

MARK 1

Jesus Hits the Ground Running

After John the Baptist prepares the way, Jesus begins His ministry. He is baptized by John and tempted by Satan. Then Jesus begins to call disciples, heal the sick, and display His power over evil spirits.

(Needed: Cleaning supplies)

Announce that you'll be cleaning up your meeting place instead of starting with a game or other "fun" activity. After listening to the groans, see how many kids dig in and get started. How many make excuses? How many do as little as possible, or try to stay out of your line of sight? When the job's done, discuss what happened. Then point out that in this chapter, Jesus begins His ministry—which will lead Him straight to the cross. How does He approach His work? Half-heartedly? Or with energy and intensity?

DATE I USED THIS SESSION _____ GROUP I USED IT WITH _____

NOTES FOR NEXT TIME_____

_____

_____

1. John the Baptist's job was to prepare people for the coming of Jesus (vss. 1-8). **Do you think his message, appearance, and diet turned people away or attracted them?** (People probably had various reactions to him. Some may have come out to hear him because he was so "weird." According to some commentators, though, John's clothes and diet were a protest against self-indulgence—not just a way to get attention.)

2. How could *you* **prepare the following people to hear about Jesus today: (a) A nice guy at school who has just moved to your town from a mostly Muslim country; (b) a teacher who likes to knock the Bible; (c) a girl at school who doesn't know anything about Jesus except that He was born in a manger?**

3. **Do you think John the Baptist was putting himself down too much when he said he wasn't worthy to untie Jesus' sandals? Would Jesus have agreed with Him?** (In a sense, John was right; Jesus is God. Yet Jesus was humble and treated people with love, not "lording" it over them.) **How do you feel when you think about Jesus' relationship to you?**

4. **If you'd watched by the Jordan River the day Jesus was baptized** (vss. 9-11), **what would you have thought about Jesus? Why? Would you have spread the word about what happened, or kept it to yourself?**

5. **Mark mentions Jesus' temptation only briefly** (vss. 12, 13) **as a step in Jesus' preparation for ministry. How can temptation prepare you to serve God better?** (When you resist temptation, it's easier to resist next time; you learn to rely on God, etc.) **What have you learned by resisting temptation?**

6. **One of the first things Jesus did was gather disciples** (vss. 14-20). **If Jesus were walking through your school or neighborhood today looking for disciples, do you think He would choose you? Why or why not?**

7. The first thing about Jesus that got people's attention was His teaching (vss. 22, 27). **But He backed up what He was saying by casting out evil spirits and healing the sick** (vss. 21-34). **What has Jesus done to get *your* attention?**

8. Why do you think Jesus was so concerned that people not be told who He really was (vss. 24, 25, 34)? (Since He was just starting His ministry, He may have wanted people to see His actions before coming to any conclusions.)

9. Jesus, the Son of God, had power that no one had seen before—or since. So why was it so important to get out of bed while it was still dark to go pray by Himself (vss. 35-37)? (Prayer must have been more to Him than an obligation or just a way to ask for things. It was Jesus' last link with His Father in heaven.) **Do you need prayer more or less than Jesus did?**

10. The leper (vss. 38-45) **hadn't been touched by a "clean" person in years, and Jesus' single touch healed him. For what problems do the kids you know need to receive the "touch" of Jesus?**

11. If you were part of a TV news crew covering the events of this chapter, which would you put first on the newscast? Second? Third? Which would provide the most dramatic videotape? Which would be most important to people in the future?

Your kids may not relate to being "fishers of men" (vss. 16, 17), but they need to see that Christ has a job for each of them. The reproducible sheet, "Not Fishers of Men," can help kids identify the kinds of unique disciples they could be. After giving kids time to fill in at least four "job titles," discuss how kids could use those interests to introduce someone to Jesus, oppose evil, or meet a hurting person's need.

"As Jesus walked beside the Sea of Galilee, he saw Simon and his brother Andrew casting a net into the lake, for they were fishermen. 'Come, follow me,' Jesus said, 'and I will make you fishers of men.' At once they left their nets and followed him" (Mark 1:16, 17).

Maybe you're not a fisherman. If Jesus wanted you to be one of His followers (and He does), what might He call you instead of a "fisher of men"? Find at least four of your interests on the following list. After each one, write what Jesus might call you to be, based on that interest. For instance, for "video games" you might write "A zapper of evil" or "A joystick of the Lord."

Video games	"A _____ of _____."	**Rock collecting**	"A _____ of _____."
Swimming	"A _____ of _____."	**Stamps**	"A _____ of _____."
Cooking	"A _____ of _____."	**Chemistry**	"A _____ of _____."
Drawing	"A _____ of _____."	**Cars**	"A _____ of _____."
Model building	"A _____ of _____."	**Pizza**	"A _____ of _____."
Basketball	"A _____ of _____."	**Special effects**	"A _____ of _____."
Computers	"A _____ of _____."	**Hair styling**	"A _____ of _____."
Music	"A _____ of _____."	**Hockey**	"A _____ of _____."
Surfing	"A _____ of _____."	**Movies**	"A _____ of _____."
T-shirts	"A _____ of _____."	**Rollerblades**	"A _____ of _____."
Speech	"A _____ of _____."	**Math**	"A _____ of _____."
Drama	"A _____ of _____."	**Aerobics**	"A _____ of _____."
Pets	"A _____ of _____."	**Science fiction**	"A _____ of _____."
Babysitting	"A _____ of _____."	**Photography**	"A _____ of _____."
Comic books	"A _____ of _____."	**Board games**	"A _____ of _____."
TV	"A _____ of _____."	**Sculpture**	"A _____ of _____."
Baseball cards	"A _____ of _____."	**Ballet**	"A _____ of _____."
Investing	"A _____ of _____."	**Demolition derby**	"A _____ of _____."
Volleyball	"A _____ of _____."	**Horses**	"A _____ of _____."
Football	"A _____ of _____."	**Bicycles**	"A _____ of _____."

MARK 2

Right Through The Roof

Jesus shows that there's a connection between His powers to heal sickness and to forgive sin. Then He calls another disciple, answers some questions about fasting, and clarifies God's intentions concerning the Sabbath.

(Needed: Heavily wrapped packages and prizes)

Bring some packages (one for each team you'll form) that you've made as difficult as possible to open. For example: A box within a box within a box, with each taped heavily, wrapped with string, etc. At your signal, teams compete to get to the small prizes inside. Then discuss: **We can work hard to win little prizes, but how hard do we work to get closer to Jesus? To bring others to Him?**

DATE I USED THIS SESSION _____ GROUP I USED IT WITH _____

NOTES FOR NEXT TIME _____

_____

_____

1. Verses 1-12 tell the story of some guys who brought a friend to Jesus—literally. **Have you ever been helpless, like the paralyzed man in the story? How did you feel?** (Examples: Having to wear a cast for a long time; lying in bed with mono or the flu.)

2. Do you have many friends who are as faithful as the ones in this story? What's the best thing a friend has ever done for you?

3. Why do you think this story is in the Bible? Is it because God wants us to punch holes in other people's roofs? (Maybe one point is that we should let nothing get between Jesus and ourselves—not physical handicaps, other people, or any other obstacle. Another might be that Jesus can forgive sin as well as heal people. As for punching holes, the paralyzed man's friends may have moved tiles or sections that could be put back.)

4. After all the effort made by these guys (vss. 4, 5), what do you think the paralyzed man felt when the only thing Jesus said was, "Son, your sins are forgiven"? (Maybe gratitude, but possibly disappointment at receiving "spiritual" healing rather than physical health.) **Do you feel satisfied that Jesus has forgiven your sins, or do you want more?**

5. At Jesus' statement, the religious leaders got upset (vss. 6, 7). *Anyone* could walk in off the street and tell someone that his or her sins were forgiven. **How did Jesus answer their doubts** (vss. 8-12)? (He performed the outward miracle of physical healing so people would believe He had performed the miracle of forgiving sins as well.) **Can you think of any other proof He might have given?**

6. Has Jesus answered *your* doubts? If so, how? If not, what would it take?

7. If you'd been in the crowd that day, what would you have wanted Jesus to do for you? Would you have tried to get His attention? If so, how?

8. Later, Jesus invited Levi (Matthew) to become a disciple (vss. 13-17). **What do you think Matthew's aim in life was the moment before Jesus came by? Do you think it changed right away? If not, how long do you think it took?**

9. One of the first things Levi did was invite Jesus to a party to meet his friends. **If our group threw a party next month to introduce your friends to Jesus, who would you invite? What would you want to do at the party?**

10. Have you ever been to a party where everyone was having a great time except for one person who wouldn't eat or laugh? **What effect did that person have on the others? What did Jesus compare this to in verses 18-20?** (People who were mourning and fasting were missing out on the "party" that Jesus was providing while He was on earth. They should have been celebrating His in-the-flesh friendship while there was still time.)

11. **How well did Jesus think His teachings would fit with those of the Pharisees (vss. 21, 22)? Explain.** (The two weren't going to mix at all. Jesus had come to fulfill everything that had been prophesied, but the Pharisees wouldn't give up their old rules and traditions.)

12. Based on Jesus' comments about the Sabbath (vss. 23-28), **do you think He was planning on adding a lot of new rules? Why or why not?** (It didn't look that way. Jesus showed that we should follow the spirit of the law, and explained what was behind it. Unlike the Pharisees, He didn't make a list of instructions on what the "minimum daily requirement" for Sabbath-keeping was.)

Hand out copies of the reproducible sheet, "Get a Little Closer," as you review the story of the paralyzed man who was carried to Jesus. After giving kids a chance to respond to it, discuss: **Why do people think they have to be perfect before they approach God? How could you ask the person you mentioned in Tip #2 to help you get closer to the Lord? Are any of your friends keeping you from getting closer to God? If so, what should you do about it?**

GET A LITTLE CLOSER

Did you get closer to Jesus last week? If not, what's your excuse? The paralyzed guy and his friends (Mark 2:1-12) didn't make excuses, and they didn't let obstacles get in their way. They wanted to be close to Jesus, and they wouldn't let anything stop them. Maybe we can take some tips from them.

TIP #1—DON'T LET WEAKNESS STOP YOU

This guy was completely paralyzed, yet he got to where Jesus was. What weaknesses keep you where you are in your relationship with Jesus, instead of moving ahead?

- ❏ "I'm just too tired."
- ❏ "I can't change my habits."
- ❏ "I tried to get up early and pray and read the Bible, but I kept falling asleep."
- ❏ Other

TIP #2—DON'T LET ALONENESS STOP YOU

The paralyzed man's friends helped him get to Jesus when he couldn't get there on his own. Who might be able to help you get closer to Jesus?

- ❏ A Christian friend (name _____
- ❏ A Christian adult (name _____).
- ❏ A Christian speaker, author, or recording artist (name _____
- ❏ Other _____).

TIP #3—DON'T LET EMBARRASSMENT STOP YOU

It wasn't exactly proper etiquette to lower a bed through somebody's roof. But it got the job done, didn't it? What fears of being embarrassed may keep you from doing what you need to do to get closer to Jesus?

- ❏ "I'd have to act super-religious."
- ❏ "My friends wouldn't like it."
- ❏ "I'd have to admit that I need help."
- ❏ Other

TIP #4—DON'T LET GUILT STOP YOU

The paralyzed guy was a sinner, but he wanted Jesus' help. Don't you? Some people try to get "good enough" on their own before they ask God for anything, but that never works. What feelings of guilt make you keep your distance from Jesus?

- ❏ "I keep doing the same sin over and over."
- ❏ "I did something really wrong once."
- ❏ "I have to be really good before Jesus would want me close to Him."
- ❏ Other

MARK 3

Lord or Lunatic?

Jesus' miracles and popularity with the crowds begin to annoy the Pharisees so much that they plot to have Him killed. Yet He continues to travel, heal, and teach. He also appoints disciples to help Him, and He teaches that those who do God's will are His extended family.

Pass out copies of the reproducible quiz, "Crazy or Not?" Have kids try to fill in the blanks to explain how the people described might *not* be crazy. Answers: (1) not if the man is an orchestra conductor and the others are playing musical instruments; (2) not if the fat and lye are combined to make soap; (3) not if the child is on fire and the man's trying to put the fire out; (4) not if it's a *bathtub* ring; (5) not if the rock is pumice, an abrasive that can clean your hands; (6) not if the man is a veterinarian, and he's listening to a sick dog panting. Note that some people can *seem* crazy until we know what's really going on. This was the case with Jesus, who was thought by some family members to be insane (Mark 3:20-22).

DATE I USED THIS SESSION _____ GROUP I USED IT WITH _____

NOTES FOR NEXT TIME _____

_____

_____

1. Have you ever been watched closely by someone? (Examples: A teacher, a suspicious store clerk, while serving as a model for an art class, etc.) **When? How did you feel?**

2. When Jesus was being watched very carefully (vss. 1-6), **how did He handle the situation?** (He turned the tables by challenging His would-be accusers. On the Sabbath, the Pharisees only approved helping the sick if the illness was life-threatening. Jesus pressed them to see if they would condemn other healing, and they couldn't.)

3. What response did Jesus have toward the stubborn Pharisees (vs. 5)? (In spite of His love and forgiveness, their hard-hearted attitude made Him angry and distressed.) **Which makes you most angry: a person who believes deeply in a non-Christian religion; someone who says there is no God; or a Christian who is hypocritical or judges people? Why?**

4. People were flocking from everywhere to see Jesus (vss. 7-11). **What made Him so popular?** (Probably not His teaching. Most probably wanted to be healed of some disease.) **What most attracts *you* to Jesus?**

5. Why didn't Jesus want people to recognize that He was the Son of God (vss. 11, 12)? (This claim would eventually lead to Jesus' death. At this early point in His ministry, He probably didn't want to make an issue of His deity.)

6. What can you tell from verses 13-19 about Jesus' disciples? (They had a variety of political views, degrees of faith in Jesus, etc.) **Which disciple do you think you might be most like? Why?**

7. How do you think Jesus felt about His family's reaction to Him (vss. 20, 21)? **How would that compare to His feelings about what the Pharisees said (vs. 22)? Have you ever been misunderstood or criticized for doing the right thing? What happened?**

8. When the Civil War threatened to destroy the United States, Abraham Lincoln quoted verse 25. Why? How would you paraphrase verses 23-27 for someone who doesn't get all that stuff about kingdoms, houses, and robbers? (Jesus couldn't have been on Satan's side; wouldn't it make more sense for Satan to be casting *in* demons rather than casting them out? Jesus had to be overcoming Satan in order to free people from his control.)

9. **Why won't God forgive someone who credits the power of the Holy Spirit to Satan instead** (vss. 28-30)? (Scholars disagree about the "unpardonable sin." But as long as people refuse to believe the power of the Holy Spirit is from God, they never put their faith in Jesus, the One of whom the Holy Spirit testifies [John 15:26]. And faith in Jesus is required for forgiveness.)

10. Based on Jesus' definition of his "family members" (vss. 31-34), **are you more like a close brother or sister, or a distant cousin?** (The more willing you are to do His will, the stronger your relationship is with Him.)

If Jesus Himself was accused of being mentally unstable, maybe we should expect similar treatment from time to time. Ask: **Have you ever felt a little crazy for believing what the Bible says? For spending time on things like church or missions trips? Was it because someone else criticized you, or for other reasons? How did you handle the situation?** Encourage kids to pray for each other, especially for times in which their own doubts or others' criticisms cause them to feel "crazy" for being Christians.

Crazy or Not?

1. You see a man in a fancy suit flapping his arms in front of a group of people who have metal tubes in their mouths. *Are they crazy?*

Not if _____

2. A girl smears a mixture of fat and lye all over her face. *Is she crazy?*

Not if _____

3. A man grabs a child, pushes him to the ground, and throws a blanket over him. *Is the man crazy?*

Not if _____

4. A woman gets rid of a brand new ring without even checking to see whether it fits her finger. *Is she crazy?*

Not if _____

5. A mom makes a kid rub a rock on his hands before he can eat. *Is she crazy?*

Not if _____

6. A man listens carefully to a pair of pants. *Is he crazy?*

Not if _____

MARK 4

Get the Point?

Jesus begins to tell parables. Most of His hearers don't figure out the meanings, but He explains most of the stories to His confused disciples. He also shows His control over the forces of nature by quieting a dangerous storm simply by speaking.

(Needed: Flashlights; prize [optional])

Bring as many flashlights as you can find. Give one or more to each person. Have kids act as if they had never seen these things before. What uses would they find for flashlights if they didn't know the intended use? If you wish, give a prize to the person who comes up with the most original "wrong" use. Later, tie this into the "lamp under . . . a bed" image (vss. 21-23) Jesus uses concerning people who are baffled by His message.

DATE I USED THIS SESSION _____ GROUP I USED IT WITH _____

NOTES FOR NEXT TIME_____

_____

_____

1. Suppose our next church service took place outdoors with the pastor sitting in a boat and telling stories to us on the shore. Would you prefer this or our standard worship service? Why?

2. If you were listening in the crowd and didn't have the secret meaning (vss. 13-20) to the story about the sower (vss. 1-9), what might you have thought it meant? (This is such a familiar story that kids might assume it is simple to decipher. Yet Jesus' own disciples had to have help [vss. 10, 13].)

3. As Jesus describes the kinds of "soils," do you recognize any of your friends being described? In what categories?

4. According to verses 10-12, why did Jesus teach in parables? Why didn't He just come right out and be more straightforward? (At times Jesus *was* very straightforward. But maybe He knew that nothing would convince many of the religious leaders of His time to repent and accept Him. Parables require faith and insight to be understood, so only real seekers would find answers.)

5. Didn't God want *everyone* to repent and be forgiven (vs. 12)? (Yes, and some religious leaders later believed that Jesus was the Son of God [Acts 6:7]. Yet Jesus knew many hard-hearted Pharisees wouldn't believe Him or seek forgiveness.)

6. Jesus is the light of the world who would eventually be revealed (vss. 21-23). When it comes to revealing Jesus to others, how brightly is your "bulb" burning: 150 watts? 60 watts? 15 watts? Or do you have a three-way bulb, changing your brightness depending on whom you're around?

7. Why will people who "have" receive more? Why will those who don't "have" lose everything (vss. 24, 25)? (Jesus isn't speaking of possessions here. He's talking about understanding His message. As we gather pieces of spiritual knowledge, the truth begins to come together for us. If we don't keep searching, we never find enough pieces to make sense.)

8. **True or false: If we don't use exactly the right words when we tell people about Jesus, nobody will become a Christian.** (False. According to verses 26-29, the good news about Jesus has a power of its own. It's important not to turn people off in the way we talk about Jesus, but God is the one who actually reaches people's hearts.)

9. **Most people expecting the Messiah were waiting for a big event, but Jesus seemed to be such a simple person. How did He explain this** (vss. 30-34)? (The kingdom was going to start small, but grow into a force to be reckoned with.) **If you're a Christian, do you feel like you're part of something big? Why or why not? How does that affect the way you live?**

10. **What part of the "calming the storm" story** (vss. 35-41) **shows that Jesus is God?** (Stopping the storm just by saying a few words.) **What shows His humanness?** (He was so tired that He fell asleep in the boat.) **When are you most glad that Jesus is God? That He knows what it's like to be human?**

The reproducible sheet, "Sow What?" will help group members see what the soil types in the parable might mean in everyday life today. Note that answers may vary and still be reasonable. Here's one set of possibilities. (Along the path: 1, 3, 6. Rocky places: 4, 7, 9. Thorny ground: 2, 8, 11. Good soil: 5, 10, 12.)

Ask: **Which soil type are you most like right now? What rocks or weeds do you need to get rid of? If you don't** *care* **what soil type you might be, what type does that probably make you?**

SOW WHAT?

ALONG THE PATH
(Mark 4:3, 4, 15)

THORNY GROUND
(Mark 4:7, 18, 19)

ROCKY PLACES
(Mark 4:5, 6, 16, 17)

GOOD SOIL
(Mark 4:8, 20)

*W*hich "soil type" goes with each of the following actions you might take? Match them up by writing each action's number on the part of the map where it belongs.

1. You fall asleep in church and don't hear a word of the sermon.

2. Being on the football team is really important to you. So is winning. All this stuff Jesus said about peacemakers and gentleness doesn't make sense on the field, so you decide Jesus is for people who just sit around and knit sweaters.

3. Your eyes sort of glaze over whenever you hear somebody reading from the Bible, and it never seems to "soak in."

4. When a friend calls you a dork for reading silently from a New Testament in study hall, you tell yourself you'll never make that mistake again.

5. You get up enough courage to tell your best friend about Jesus, and she/he just says, "I'll think about it, OK?"

6. Your Sunday school teacher asks you to write a rap based on Mark 4 this week, but you forget.

7. Becoming a Christian sounded pretty good a year ago, when you were so depressed over your parents' divorce. But now that you're starting to feel better, you're less and less interested in things like youth group and praying.

8. Given a choice between going on a summer missions trip and making an extra $250 to buy a new CD player, you pick the money.

9. You come home from a great week at a Christian camp and tell your mom that you've "asked Jesus into your heart." When she laughs and says, "You've either got a pretty small Jesus or a pretty big heart," you start to think the whole thing does sound kind of dumb.

10. After hearing a missionary talk about feeding the hungry, you convince your family to "adopt" a Central American orphan by sending money to the orphanage each month.

11. You've been trying to get your boyfriend/girlfriend to go to a Christian concert, hoping he/she will accept Jesus as you did a few months ago. But he/she isn't interested. Forced to choose between Jesus and a relationship you can see and feel, you dump Jesus.

12. While helping out at vacation Bible school, you tell a 10-year-old girl how to accept Jesus as her Savior—and she does it.

MARK 5

No Job Too Big

Jesus demonstrates His unlimited power in several ways. First, he heals a demon-possessed man by sending the demons into a herd of pigs. Then he heals a woman who has had a bleeding problem for twelve years. Finally, He brings a dead girl back to life.

(Needed: Prizes [optional])

Play "Anatomy." Have everyone get a partner. Form two groups, with one person from each partnership in each group. The first group forms a circle; the other group forms a larger circle around the first one. The inner group begins to walk in a clockwise direction, and the outer group walks counter-clockwise. Whenever you like, shout out two body parts (such as "Right ear to left heel"). Immediately each person in the center circle tries to touch his or her right ear to the partner's left heel. No need to stay in circles; a mad scramble is much better! The last pair to "make the connection" is out. Continue until only one (winning) pair is left. (Note: If your group is small, have each pair walk in its own little circle.) Later, show what was "won" by the woman who touched her finger to Jesus' clothes (vss. 25-34).

DATE I USED THIS SESSION _____ GROUP I USED IT WITH _____

NOTES FOR NEXT TIME_____

_____

_____

1. Have you ever seen anyone who wasn't in control of his or her mind or actions? How did you feel around that person?

2. The possessed man in this story (vss. 1-20) couldn't be controlled, even for his own protection. His actions were self-destructive (vs. 5). What kinds of things make kids feel "out of control" today? Have you ever felt that way? Have you ever felt things around you were out of control? What did you do about it?

3. The demons in the man recognized Jesus at once. What was their fear? (They probably didn't want to be condemned eternally before God's final judgment.)

4. Imagine, if you can, 2,000 pigs rushing into a lake and drowning themselves (vss. 11-13). As a group, can you do an impression of what that might have sounded like? If you'd been tending the pigs, what would have been your reaction?

5. Jesus brought this man back under control. What does that tell you about times when you feel out of control? (No feelings, no situations are too tough for Jesus to get control of. We have to be willing to let Him have control, though.)

6. When people saw the man in his *right* mind, they got scared (vs. 15). Do you ever assume that certain people can't or won't change? Is that fair? Give examples.

7. How could you do what Jesus told the healed man to do (vss. 18, 19)? Is it harder or easier to talk to your family about God than it is to talk to others? Why?

8. Later, Jesus suddenly stopped and wanted to know who had touched Him (vss. 21-34). If you had been the "culprit," would you have confessed? Why?

9. Have you ever wanted something from God, but didn't want to "bother" Him? Why? Do you think Jesus was bothered by this woman? (No. Jesus encouraged people who showed faith in Him.)

10. How would you have felt if you'd been Jairus, (a) begging the controversial Jesus for help; (b) hearing that your daughter had died; (c) right after Jesus said, "Don't be afraid, only believe"; (d) when Jesus said, "The child is not dead, but asleep"; (e) when your daughter stood up; and (f) when Jesus gave orders not to tell anyone what had happened?

11. What might have happened if word had gotten around right away that Jesus could bring people back from the dead? (He would have been deluged with requests to bring back to life practically everyone who had ever died.) What might happen today if God routinely answered people's prayers to bring their dead loved ones back to life? (One possibility: maybe people wouldn't be motivated to accept Jesus, thinking they'd never face judgment or punishment.)

12. Right now, do you have a "crowd" of problems (like the demon-possessed man); one big, long-lasting problem (like the woman); or a wish that someone else's problem would be solved (like Jairus)? (You may want to compile a group prayer list if kids are willing to share.)

Have some fun with the reproducible sheet, "Soap Opera Roundup." Note that problems from loneliness to drinking to self-image are woven into the plot summaries. After kids follow the instructions, discuss the results as they're willing. Ask: **Do you believe Jesus wants to help you today as much as He wanted to help the people in Mark 5? Why or why not? If no problem is too hard for God, what stands in the way of solving your problems? Why might God choose to let you live with a problem instead of wiping it away?**

SOAP OPERA ROUND UP

Here's what happened last week on all those soap operas you love (or hate). Nothing but problems, problems, problems. After looking at Mark 5, circle all the problems on this page that you think would be too tough for Jesus to solve. Underline all the problems that are a little like the ones you face. Then check to see how many you've both circled *and* underlined. What does that tell you?

ALL MY CHIP DIPS

Arnie decides to go to college, but doesn't know which one to apply to. He orders college catalogs, but then remembers he can't read. Erika wishes Arnie would fall in love with her, but he seems not to notice her. So she spends an afternoon reading catalogs to him—but mistakenly brings the ones from Sears and L. L. Bean, and Arnie gets mad. Bruno overhears Erika reading catalogs and wishes he could get some nice clothes like the ones she's reading about, but his family never seems to have enough money. Maybe that's because Bruno's father can only find minimum wage jobs. Or maybe it's because Bruno eats 57 pounds of groceries a day.

THE EDGE OF NIGHTGOWNS

Kabel, the new guy in town, doesn't know anybody. Then he meets Drusilla at the local animal shelter. Drusilla has always wanted a pet, but her father won't let her have one—or anything else she wants. So she just sits in front of the cages every Saturday and looks depressed. Kabel wants to start a conversation with Drusilla, but doesn't know how. He's embarrassed by the way he looks. But he does a great impression of a German shepherd, and that makes Drusilla laugh. Unfortunately, it irritates the German shepherds, who eat all the Chihuahuas.

THE YOUNG AND THE BRAINLESS

Garth is flunking all his courses except Small Blimp Repair. One of his teachers, Mrs. Hatchetson, has always seemed to dislike him. Apparently she has turned the other teachers against him, except for Mr. Fleameyer in Small Blimp Repair. Garth confronts Mrs. Hatchetson in the cafeteria. In the heat of the moment he calls her a small blimp, and is sent to the principal's office. Only the love of Alicia can keep Garth from being expelled. Too bad Alicia has moved away to Antarctica, where she has started to go out with a penguin.

GENERAL CUSTER HOSPITAL

When a close relative gets sick, Krystle is worried. Dr. Buzz reassures her, but he seems to have a drinking problem. Krystle asks Nurse Rachel for advice, but Rachel is too busy. It seems the nurse has signed up for too many activities, and she is exhausted. Krystle takes her fears to a clergyman, who quotes some Bible verses she doesn't understand. Finally she goes to the only one who has ever been able to help her—a Chihuahua at the local animal shelter. When she learns that the Chihuahuas have been eaten by the German shepherds, she goes into a coma and is unable to remember her locker combination.

MARK 6

The Rejected Prophets Society

Jesus' ministry takes a more somber tone as He is rejected by His hometown and sends out the twelve disciples with some words of warning. The death of John the Baptist is also recorded. Yet Jesus shows who is still in control of everything as He feeds five thousand hungry people and walks on water.

(Needed: Calculator)

Say: **Suppose a billionaire walked into this room right now and gave each of you a choice. He says, "Here are some contracts. You can sign Contract #1, for which I will give you 1¢ today, 2¢ tomorrow, 4¢ the next day, each day doubling your amount for thirty days. By Day 20 you will have $5,242. 88. Or you can sign Contract #2, for which you will receive *one million dollars* on Day 30. But you have to tell me right now which contract you want."** Ask for an immediate show of hands. Then let kids use the calculator to see which is the better deal. (The thirty-day total of the first option should come to $5,368,709.12.) Compare to the "multiplication" of the loaves and fishes described in this chapter.

DATE I USED THIS SESSION _____ GROUP I USED IT WITH _____

NOTES FOR NEXT TIME _____

_____

_____

Q&A

1. Do your parents or teachers ever talk about how great other kids are, while seeming to overlook your own good qualities? Give some examples and tell how it makes you feel.

2. When Jesus went back to his hometown (vss. 1-6), people were not very impressed with Him. Why not? (They'd known Him as a child, and apparently He hadn't seemed like anyone special. When, as an adult, He began to teach and perform miracles, the hometown people weren't willing to adjust their thinking.)

3. In verse 5, is Jesus most like (a) Superman being hurt by Kryptonite, (b) a person trying to sell refrigerators in the Arctic, or (c) somebody trying to squeeze blood from a stone? Why? (Probably [b]; people there just didn't have faith in Him, and He healed people who had faith.)

4. If you had been one of the twelve disciples being sent out by Jesus (vss. 7-13), what would you have liked about the assignment? (Possibly the ability to perform miracles; Jesus' trust in you; the chance to help others, etc.) What might you not have liked? (Rejection; living by faith on the "bare minimum"; confronting people, etc.)

5. John the Baptist was dead (vss. 14-29). Herod had ordered John to be killed, even though he liked to listen to John and knew John was a righteous man. So why kill him? (Herod didn't want to look weak in front of his guests, Herodias, or her daughter.)

6. What's one thing you've done just to look good in front of other people? What have you done just because someone dared you? How about feats to impress a person of the opposite sex? Do you regret any of these?

7. Have you ever been desperate just to be by yourself for a while? As hard as Jesus tried, people followed Him everywhere. How did He feel about that? (Vss. 30-34—He wasn't annoyed. He had compassion on them.)

8. Jesus wasn't only concerned with people's spiritual needs. He also knew they were hungry and needed something to eat (vss. 35-37). How well does our group meet both the spiritual and physical needs of the people in it? Of people outside of it?

9. If you had the power to heal people and feed thousands, what's the first thing you would do? If the devil had that power, how do you think he would use it?

10. Still wanting to be alone, Jesus sent the disciples across the water while He went to pray (vss. 45-52). He caught up with them in an unusual way. If you were one of the disciples at this point, what thoughts would be going through your head? (Things were happening too fast for the disciples. They were still confused about how Jesus had fed the 5,000 when He suddenly proved He could walk on water. They didn't have enough faith to handle all this.)

11. Who are you more like: (a) the disciples, struggling to understand more about how Jesus operated, or (b) the others who simply wanted something from Jesus, such as healing [vss. 55, 56]), **and didn't care how He did it? Explain.**

The reproducible sheet, "Five Plus Two," will help kids focus on skills they can turn over to God, and the possible results. After having fun with the first five questions, give kids time to fill in the rest of the sheet. Then discuss: **Which of these abilities are you really willing to let God use? Which are you still holding on to?**

What's the biggest thing you could buy in a supermarket with five bucks and two quarters?

_____

What's the best entertainment you could rent in a video store that would last five hours and two minutes (or less)?

_____

What's the most important letter you could write with five pieces of paper and two pencils?

_____

What's the farthest you could run in five minutes and two seconds?

_____

What's the most people you could feed with five loaves of bread and two fish?

_____

What if the owner of the five loaves and two fish (Mark 6:35-44) hadn't been willing to part with them? ("Forget it. I'm hungry. Go get your own lunch.") In the hands of Jesus, that simple gift was multiplied until more than 5,000 people were fed.

If you're willing to let Jesus work with what you have, stand back! And find some baskets, because there's going to be more than you can handle.

What's the best God might be able to do if He could use five of your abilities (no matter how small) for two hours?

	ABILITY	TWO HOUR-TASK	BEST RESULT I COULD HOPE FOR
1.			
2.			
3.			
4.			
5.			

MARK 7

Clean and Dirty

Jesus confronts the Pharisees regarding the things that truly make a person "clean" or "unclean." Then He meets a non-Jewish woman who shows tremendous insight and faith. Finally, He heals a deaf and mute man.

(Needed: Refreshments, plates, utensils)

Lay out some refreshments, plates, and utensils. Gather around to eat. Have someone pray. As kids prepare to dig in, stop them and insist that they go wash their hands first. When they reassemble, stop them again and make them wash the cups and plates. When that's over, suddenly "remember" that this is the time when your church celebrates an official "holy day" (a missionary's birthday, the anniversary of when the pastor came to your church, or some such excuse) by fasting for an hour. When kids threaten to riot, explain that you're just doing what the Pharisees (to be studied in this chapter) probably would have done. Then serve the refreshments.

DATE I USED THIS SESSION _____ GROUP I USED IT WITH _____

NOTES FOR NEXT TIME _____

_____

_____

1. What do people say about your eating habits? What do you find fascinating about the eating habits of other people in this group?

2. The Pharisees were very particular about their eating procedures (vss. 1-4). **Why did they place so much emphasis on being "clean" in the first place?** (It was a religious term showing that they had done everything necessary to be presentable to God.)

3. The Pharisees hadn't been so careful to keep their inner selves as clean as their outer selves (vss. 5-8). Jesus said their hearts were far from God. **When is your heart closest to God? Farthest?**

4. Jesus said the Pharisees' worship was "in vain." **How would you feel if your thoughts were flashed on a screen in front of the church during (a) the singing; (b) the prayer; and (d) the offering? What parts of your worship tend to be real, and which tend to be "in vain"?**

5. The Pharisees taught "Honor your father and mother." But they let people claim that money needed by parents was devoted to God—even if it really wasn't (vss. 9-13). **What do you think the Pharisees would think about the way you treat your parent(s)?**

6. Jesus explained that it wasn't the digestive tract that makes a person unclean (vss. 14-23). **What *does* make us unclean?** (Wrong thoughts and sinful desires we hold in our hearts.) **Have you ever felt "dirty" because you did something wrong? Have you ever felt "clean" because you were forgiven? What was it like?**

7. Of the thirteen evils listed in verses 20-23, **which three do you think are most common in your school? Which three are least common? How would life at school change if all thirteen of these disappeared?**

8. A woman found Jesus and asked for help for her demon-possessed daughter. **Do you think Jesus' answer** (vs. 27) **was rude? Explain.** (The "children" He referred to could have been the disciples or the Jewish people. As a "dog" [a family pet], the woman was supposed to wait her turn to be "fed." But she realized that Jesus would not let the "dogs" go hungry, and that He could help her *and* His own people. Jesus gave the woman an opportunity to show her faith, and she did.)

9. **Why do you think Jesus took the deaf-mute man away from the crowd** (vss. 31-37) **to heal him?** (Maybe He didn't want it to seem like a circus; maybe the man was self-conscious; maybe Jesus was still trying to keep a low profile.)

If you had gone to Jesus for healing, would it bother you if a crowd were watching?

10. **Why would Jesus put His fingers in the man's ears, spit, touch the man's tongue, look up to heaven, and say, "Be opened"? Why not just wave His hand?** (Perhaps Jesus was helping the man, who couldn't hear, to understand what was happening. Jesus' actions seemed to say, "I'm going to fix your ears and your tongue. The power comes from God." Maybe the man could lip-read the command, "Be opened!")

11. **If you received a miraculous healing and Jesus asked you to keep it quiet, would you? Explain.**

Pass out the reproducible sheet, "Spirit Subtraction," and have kids figure out the word puzzles. Answers to puzzles: (FAKING IT; HYPOCRISY; GOING THROUGH THE MOTIONS; BOREDOM; RITUAL; RESENTMENT TOWARD GOD; LIFELESSNESS; JUDGING OTHERS.) Then discuss kids' answers to the questions. Help them to see that God wants the kind of obedience that comes from loving and respecting Him—not the kind that says, "I'll follow Your little rules if I have to, but I won't like it."

Spirit SUBTRACTION

Jesus said the Pharisees had "let go of the commands of God and are holding on to the traditions of men." What happens when you take away the *spirit* of a command (God's reason and feeling behind it, and the real results He wants) and you're left with only a hollow shell of a rule? Try taking away the word "SPIRIT" from each of the following and see what you're left with. (You may need to rearrange spaces, too.) Then answer the questions.

FASKIPIN GRIITT
When it comes to your faith, who are you most likely to do this around?

SHYPOPIRCIRISTY
What's one of the worst examples you've ever seen of this? (No names, please.)

GOSPINGITH ROURGH IT HEMTOTIONS
When are you most likely to do this in church?

BORSEPIDORMIT
What two "rules" about being a Christian come to mind when you see this word?

SPIRITUALRIT
What happens when you do this over and over?

RESSPENTIMERNT TIOWARDG TOD
Do you really believe the Lord has your best interests at heart? Why or why not?

LISPFELIRESSINESTS
Do you think God wants an army of zombies? Why or why not?

JUSPIDGIN GROTIHERTS
How does concentrating on the details of rules lead to this?

MARK 8

Bread and Fish Again?

After recently feeding the five thousand, Jesus again performs a miracle to provide food for a large crowd. His disciples are still slow to comprehend the full significance of the things He is doing, though Peter receives some insight into Jesus' real identity. Jesus also heals a blind man and predicts His own death.

Before the session, cut copies of "Megabyte Memory," the reproducible sheet, on the dotted line. Pass out just the top half (Version 1.0). Give kids thirty seconds to look over the numbers. Collect the sheets. Then hand out the bottom half (Version 2.0). Kids are to circle all the numbers that don't match the first version. After revealing the correct answers, see who displayed the best memory. Use this as an introduction to the first question in "Q & A."

DATE I USED THIS SESSION _____ GROUP I USED IT WITH _____

NOTES FOR NEXT TIME _____

_____

_____

Q&A

1. Have you ever tried and tried to learn or memorize something, but for some reason it just wouldn't soak in? What do you think the problem was?

2. How does the disciples' answer in Matthew 8:4 show that they had a learning problem, too? (Not long before, Jesus had challenged His disciples to feed a crowd of more than five thousand people [Mark 6:37]. They couldn't do it with only five loaves and two fish. Jesus showed them how it was done, and now gives them another opportunity—this time with a little more food and fewer people [vss. 1-13]. But the disciples have just as little faith now as they did last time.)

3. How do you think Jesus felt when His disciples wouldn't increase their faith? (Disappointed; frustrated; He probably expected it.)

4. Immediately following the feeding of the four thousand, the Pharisees asked Jesus to give them a sign (vss. 11-13). What do you think about their request? How do you think Jesus felt after performing a repeat of one of the greatest miracles ever seen and *then* being asked for a sign?

5. What are the most obvious signs that God is alive? Why do so many people ignore them? (They think more "modern" explanations are better; they think that if God existed He wouldn't allow anyone to suffer, etc. In the meantime, they ignore the beauty of creation, the good things He has provided in life, the privilege of forgiveness and salvation, etc.)

6. Using a loaf of bread as an object lesson, Jesus told the disciples, "Watch out for the yeast of the Pharisees" (vs. 15). The disciples had no idea what He meant. Do you? (It was like saying, "One bad apple spoils the whole bunch." The yeast [evil] of the religious leaders could spread to all the Jewish people if not confronted and corrected.)

7. Whose "yeast" do you need to watch out for? (Cults; materialism; the New Age movement; the occult, etc.)

8. When Jesus first touched the blind man (vss. 22-26), the man still couldn't see well. Another touch cleared things up. Has Jesus ever "cleared something up" for you—a problem, a mistaken idea? Did it happen all at once, or in stages? How?

9. The blind man could have left after the first touch, saying, "Thanks. That's a little better." But he was honest with Jesus and received complete healing. How might each of the following settle for less than Jesus can provide: (a) a girl who lives in a small town where there aren't many Christian guys; (b) a guy who uses drugs and figures he'll never be able to change?

10. The good news was that Peter (and soon others) would begin to recognize Jesus as the Christ—the Savior of the world (vss. 27-30). The bad news was that He would have to die to accomplish what He had come for. Peter didn't want to hear such talk (vss. 31-33). **Why was Jesus' response so harsh?** (It was God's will for Jesus to die. Anyone who opposed that plan stood in the way. Maybe Peter's lack of support was also making it that much harder for Jesus to give up His life.)

11. Jesus would willingly give up His life, but His followers would also be expected to give up certain things as well (vss. 34-38). **Have you given up anything for Jesus? If so, what? If not, why not?**

Say: **When Jesus asked the disciples a tough question, they didn't have answers ready. Everything Jesus said and did was new to them. If you've been in the church for long, maybe you hardly have to think to give the "right" answers to Bible questions. But if Jesus were asking you these questions today** *for the first time,* **what would you say? Write your answers,** *based only on your own life experiences.* **(1) "Who do people say I [Jesus] am?" (2) "But what about you? Who do you say I [Jesus] am?" (3) "What good is it for a man to gain the whole world, yet forfeit his soul? Or what can a man give in exchange for his soul?"** After kids have time to write, discuss the results.

MEGABYTE MEMORY

VERSION 1.0

56	12	74	8	32	20
6	91	88	10	40	14
59	27	4	19	65	8
77	6	13	34	2	21

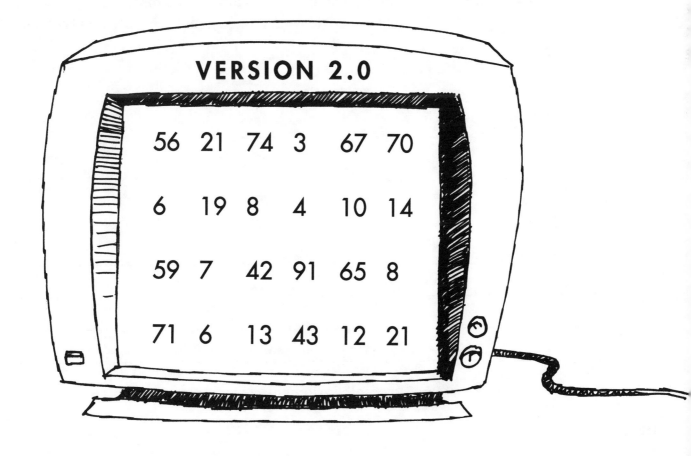

VERSION 2.0

56	21	74	3	67	70
6	19	8	4	10	14
59	7	42	91	65	8
71	6	13	43	12	21

I'm Not the Greatest

Jesus' transfiguration is witnessed by three of His disciples. The other disciples, in the meantime, are unable to cast out a demon. After criticizing the lack of faith around Him, Jesus heals the possessed boy. He again predicts His death and then settles an argument among the disciples. New disciples appear, healing in the name of Jesus. And Jesus gives some shocking advice for how to avoid hell.

Say that you're considering appointing an "emperor" for your group—someone who'll determine what activities you do, how the group spends its money, who does which jobs, etc. Let as many volunteers as possible give "campaign speeches" to explain why they would be best qualified for the position. Later, recall their comments as you discuss Jesus' teaching that those who would be first must be the servants of all.

DATE I USED THIS SESSION _____ GROUP I USED IT WITH _____

NOTES FOR NEXT TIME _____

_____

_____

1. What's the biggest change you've ever seen in a person? (A Christian conversion; a successful diet; a loner who begins to date regularly, etc.)

2. The disciples had seen Jesus perform a lot of miracles, but they had seen nothing like His transfiguration (vss. 1-13). What do you think was so important about this event? (This was something that happened *to* Jesus, rather than something He performed; it showed Him [for a time] beyond the limitations of His human body; it showed His relationship to Moses and Elijah; He received the "endorsement" of God the Father, etc.)

3. Why do you think Jesus took along three of the disciples? (Though He didn't want them to say anything about it right away [vs. 9], it was important that they remember this after Jesus eventually rose from the dead.)

4. After everything Jesus had done and said to this point, the disciples still had no idea what He meant when He said He was going to rise from the dead (vs. 10). Do you think you would have done a better job of understanding? Worse? About the same? Explain.

5. While three of the disciples had been on the mountain with Jesus, the others had found themselves in the middle of an argument. They had been unable to remove an evil spirit from a boy (vss. 14-29). How do you think they felt? How do you think they felt when Jesus said what He did in verse 19?

6. The boy's father began with a low level of faith: "If you can do anything, . . . help us" (vs. 22). Jesus quickly let him know there were no "ifs" concerning His power. Have you ever prayed for anything, yet secretly doubted it would be done? What might happen if you were as honest with God as the man was in verse 24?

7. According to Jesus, there is tremendous power in praying (vs. 29). What difference do you think praying in advance could make in the following situations: (a) going on a first date with a person you really like; (b) talking to a friend who wants to commit suicide; (c) confronting a parent who has been abusing you; (d) planning a youth group party for non-Christian friends?

8. Even as Jesus was preparing to lay His life down to save mankind (vss. 30-32), the disciples were involved in a "Who's Number One?" discussion. When you're at home, do you act more like the disciples, or like the model Jesus presented (vss. 36, 37)? Explain.

9. The disciples felt threatened when other people began to accomplish results in the name of Jesus [vss. 38-41]. How would you feel if you heard that another church youth group down the street was growing three times as fast as yours? How do you think Jesus would feel about it?

10. Looking back at your actions toward younger kids during the past month or so, do you think you should be wearing a millstone necklace (vs. 42)? Explain.

11. What are some ways to obey Jesus' strong words (vss. 43-50) **without actually having to use a sharp instrument?** (Whenever temptation strikes, we can act *as if* we do not have hands, feet, eyes, etc. The pain of missing out on the temptation is small compared to the reality of hell.)

The reproducible sheet, "First or Last?" will help kids think through their status—and their attitudes toward others "in line." Help kids see that no matter where they seem to stand in line, they're valuable to you, to your group, and to God. Spend some time in prayer, letting kids talk silently to God about their attitudes concerning their places in line.

FIRST OR LAST

Do nice guys finish last? Does the one with the most toys win? Or was Jesus right when He said, "If anyone wants to be first, he must be the very last, and the servant of all"?

In each of the following categories, circle the person in line who best represents where you feel you are.

LAST   **FIRST**

Popularity at school

Making good grades

Musical ability

Athletic ability

Obedience to God

Looks

Self-confidence

Prayer/devotional life

Financial status

Sense of humor

Note: Being first in these things is not necessarily bad. And being last is not necessarily more spiritual. But what's your attitude toward your position? If you're near the front of a line, do you feel better than somebody else? If you're near the back, do you resent those in front of you?

Put a check mark to the left of any category in which you could use a change in attitude.

MARK 10

Who's on First?

Jesus provides insight on divorce and childlikeness, and is saddened when a potential new disciple can't quite put God's kingdom before his other priorities. Later, Jesus again predicts His death, referees a power struggle among the disciples, and heals a blind man.

(Needed: Beanbag chair; paper plate; string)

Tell kids you're going to have a beanbag tossing contest. Your target is a paper plate with a six-inch-diameter hole cut in it; the plate is suspended from the ceiling by a string. Explain that the object is to toss the beanbag through the hole. Have kids line up, with the tossing line about ten feet from the plate. Then hand the first participant a beanbag *chair* you've been hiding. When kids protest the impossibility of getting the chair through the hole, make the tie-in to the "camel . . . through the eye of a needle" idea in verse 25.

DATE I USED THIS SESSION _____ GROUP I USED IT WITH _____

NOTES FOR NEXT TIME _____

_____

_____

1. Which of the following statements best sums up your attitude toward divorce? (a) Nobody should get divorced—no matter what happens. (b) Divorce is much too common, and should be considered only in extreme cases like adultery or abuse. (c) Acceptance of divorce should help put people's minds at rest as they get married, because if the marriage doesn't work out, they can always get a divorce. (d) People will never change, so we should accept a high divorce rate as a fact of life.

2. What were Jesus' instructions on divorce (vss. 1-12)? How might His comments influence your dating and possible marriage? (Jesus says that marriage should be for life. God joins marriage partners together, so we shouldn't take a casual attitude toward engagement and marriage.)

3. What do you think Jesus said when He blessed the children in verses 13-16? If you'd been blessed by Jesus as a child, how do you think it might affect the rest of your life?

4. How does a little child "receive the kingdom of God" (vs. 15)? (Most children seem more willing to believe in Jesus, and to be open about their feelings toward Him, than many adults do.) **How do we keep each other from being like children in our acceptance of Jesus?** (We might make fun of "wrong" answers, "weird" expressions of faith, or being "too" in love with Jesus.)

5. Suppose you'd been right behind the rich man (vss. 17-22) to ask Jesus if you could follow Him. After hearing the conversation between the man and Jesus, would you still have asked to follow? Explain.

6. Couldn't Jesus have let the man become a disciple first and later convinced him to sell all he had and give to the poor? (Maybe, but the man's wealth seemed to be standing in the way of His willingness to really obey Jesus. Money—or at least wholehearted obedience—probably would have continued to be a problem.)

7. Why is it so important to put God before money and possessions (vss. 22-27)? (They easily become a wall between us and God; He isn't interested in second place.) **If you don't struggle with wealth being first, what other interests tend to push God out of the top spot in your life?**

8. Jesus kept trying to prepare the disciples for His death, but they just didn't get it. In fact, they started a big argument over who would get special privileges (vss. 32-45). **Have you ever failed to notice that someone close to you was going through a very hard time? If you could relive that time, what would you change?**

9. Who "lords it over you" these days (vs. 42)? Who is most like a servant to you (vs. 43)? Which of these would you like to imitate, and why?

10. Bartimaeus, the blind man, received his sight mainly because he wouldn't shut up when everyone told him to be quiet (vss. 46-52). **What happens (or would happen) in our group if someone talked "too much" about Jesus or about a certain prayer request? Do you usually feel more like Bartimaeus or like those who told him to be quiet? Why?**

Pass out copies of the reproducible sheet, "You versus the Rich Guy." Have kids fill in first-column answers from verses 17-22, and second-column answers from their own lives. They should discover that the man could easily have passed the first three tests, yet was tripped up on #4—obedience. Ask: **Is this the case with you, too? What would you find almost impossible to give up—even for Jesus? What might Jesus say to you today if you were in the rich man's place?**

You vs The Rich Guy

A lot of people wanted to follow Jesus around. But to train His disciples, Jesus had to limit the number who could follow Him around *all* the time.

One outstanding "draft pick" for discipleship was the rich young man described in Mark 10:17-22. Use the chart below to compare yourself to this person.

	THE RICH GUY	YOU
TEST #1: ATTITUDE Do you really want to be closer to Jesus? Do you really want eternal life?		
TEST #2: BEHAVIOR Do you follow God's established standards, such as the Ten Commandments? Do you have a good working knowledge of Scripture so that you know what God expects of you?		
TEST #3: RELATIONSHIP Do you show the proper respect for Jesus? Does He love you?		
TEST #4: OBEDIENCE Are you willing to do whatever Jesus asks of you? If not, what are the areas where you wish to hold back?		

MARK 11

Hosannas and a Housecleaning

Jesus makes His "triumphal entry" into Jerusalem, receiving praise from the people He rides past. He teaches a spiritual lesson by withering a fig tree, clears the money changers out of the temple, and again confronts the Pharisees who question His authority.

Announce that you're going to have a spur-of-the-moment gift exchange. Kids will give each other gifts—but only from their pockets or purses, or what they can make in two minutes from stuff found on the floor. Then note and evaluate the sincerity and quality of these gifts. This activity will lead you into the study of Jesus' triumphal entry, when people honored Him with whatever they could find.

DATE I USED THIS SESSION _____ GROUP I USED IT WITH _____

NOTES FOR NEXT TIME _____

_____

_____

1. If a stranger walked up and asked for your car (or bicycle) and said, "The Lord needs it and will send it back here shortly" (vss. 1-6), how would you respond?

2. Have you ever "loaned" anything to Jesus—allowed anything of yours to be used for His work? What happened?

3. How do you think the two disciples felt about their assignment (vss. 1-6)? When does following Jesus seem most risky or embarrassing to you?

4. This was a spur-of-the-moment parade; the disciples hadn't put up posters the week before. Do you think our group should be more spur-of-the-moment, or should we prepare more for events? Do you think we trust God enough to take care of the way things turn out in our group?

5. Besides the cloaks and branches, Jesus got verbal praise from the people (vss. 9-11). Other than singing songs in church, how can you praise God? What could our group do to praise God with as much energy as the people who shouted, "Hosanna"? (Sing some fun songs that talk about God's attributes; put on a play; stage a parade, etc.)

6. Why was Jesus so annoyed at the fig tree that had no fruit (vss. 12-14, 20, 21)? (When all the leaves come out on fig trees, the figs should also be growing. From a distance, the tree looked fruitful. But up close, it wasn't.)

7. When others see you "from a distance," do you think they see you as "religious" or not? What happens when they get closer? Outside of church, how "close" does someone have to get to you to find out whether you're a Christian?

8. Why do you think Jesus got so angry when He went to the temple (vss. 15-19)? (The people had just praised Him in person—spontaneously and from the heart. But what He found at the temple, the "headquarters" of their organized religion, was heartless and phony and had perverted the worship of God.)

9. If you believed a practice at your church was wrong, what would you do? Why?

10. Do verses 22-24 sound like a "magic formula" to you? How is obeying these verses different from saying some "magic words" to get what you want? ("Magic words" supposedly force some supernatural power to give you what you want. Jesus' instructions are about having faith in God, who can't be forced into anything, but who is willing to reward great faith with things that are right for us.)

11. What does verse 25 have to do with verses 22-24? (All these verses are about how God sees our hearts when we pray. If we don't really believe, or if we haven't forgiven others, we aren't in a position to ask God for things.)

12. The Pharisees kept questioning Jesus' authority, but were afraid to push too hard because of His popularity with the people (vss. 27-33). What do you think attracted people to Jesus more than to the Pharisees? (His compassion, authority, fresh teachings, etc.) What about *you* might help attract people to Jesus?

Use the reproducible sheet, "Apple-cation," to help kids think about how productive they are for God. Discuss the results as kids are willing. Ask: **What other kinds of apples might describe how you're doing in these areas? Unripe apples? Apples covered with pesticides? Applesauce?** Challenge kids to care about being fruitful instead of just finding a comfortable corner of the "orchard." Keep in mind, though, that most of their "mature fruit" may come later.

Apple-cation

Jesus wasn't happy with the fruitless fig tree (Mark 11:12-14). Christians are intended to produce spiritual "fruit," too—by "growing" to be more like Jesus, and by "planting the seed" of the Gospel in the lives of other people.

How's your "fruit" in the 10 areas listed below? Growing like crazy? Small and wormy? Not there at all? Fake as wax fruit? Draw a line from each item on the list to the section of the tree that describes how you're doing.

1. Caring about others and not just myself

2. Serving people instead of using them

3. Being patient

4. Controlling what I say when I'm angry

5. Learning more from the Bible on my own

6. Being thankful and praising God

7. Enjoying the fact that I belong to Jesus

8. Doing the right thing even if other kids think it's stupid

9. Helping others to believe in Jesus

10. Getting along with my parent(s)

MARK 12

Sticky Questions

Jesus has several verbal confrontations with the Pharisees and other religious leaders. He tells a parable that makes them uneasy, foils their attempt to force Him to choose between loyalty to government and to God, answers difficult questions, and finally witnesses a noteworthy example of giving.

(Needed: Building materials; team prize)

Bring an assortment of building materials (boxes, string, tape, wire, glue, stray pieces of hardware such as hinges and springs, etc.). Form teams. Each team is to build "a better mousetrap" (an improvement over the conventional design) in five minutes, using the materials at hand. Give a prize for the best (or the most complicated) trap. Then explain that you'll be studying the religious leaders' repeated tries to "trap" Jesus with their questions.

DATE I USED THIS SESSION _____ GROUP I USED IT WITH _____

NOTES FOR NEXT TIME _____

_____

_____

1. What's the most fragile, expensive, or precious thing you ever had to take care of for someone else? How was caring for someone else's property different from caring for your own?

2. What points do you think Jesus was trying to get across in the Parable of the Tenants (vss. 1-12) that still apply to us? (Jesus will return one day to judge the wicked; we have certain responsibilities while we await His return; when we begin to think we can control our own lives, we are mistaken, etc.)

3. How many minutes in a year do you suppose you spend thinking about the return of Jesus? How might that affect what you do?

4. What are some of the things people today are expected to give "Caesar" (vss. 13-17)? (Loyalty; income tax; sales tax; driver's license fees; military service; jury duty, etc.)

5. How do some people try to avoid giving things to the government? (Cheating on taxes; claiming to be eligible for benefits they shouldn't get, etc.) **What do you think about people who protest laws by not paying taxes or by refusing to obey in other ways?** (Contrast protests based on sincere faith with those based solely on frustration with the government.)

6. What is God's (vs. 17)? How do some people try to avoid giving Him what belongs to Him? (Everything belongs to God. Whenever we try to keep ourselves or our possessions out of His control, we're trying to rob Him. Part of obeying God is obeying the laws of the land, except when doing so would cause us to disobey God [see Romans 13:1-7].)

7. Do you ever wonder about life after death, with all the stories of near-death experiences (seeing bright lights, coming back from a wonderful place, seeing relatives long dead, etc.)? Based on Jesus' comments in verses 24-27, what do you think He would tell you if you asked what life after death is like? (He might repeat what He said in vs. 25, but His comment in verse 27 may indicate that we should focus on the reality of the here and now instead of getting obsessed with the hereafter.)

8. Look at the Ten Commandments in Exodus 20. How would you rank them in "greatness" from 1 to 10? How does your answer compare with Mark 10:28-34?

9. Compare verses 35-37 with Psalm 110:1. Because Jesus knew Scripture so well, He could pull out a verse, ask an intriguing question, and "delight" the crowd. Does the word "delight" fit your reaction to Jesus' teachings? If not, what word fits?

10. Jesus said to "watch out" for the teachers of the law (vss. 38-40). **Was their desire to be honored wrong in itself? Or was there a deeper problem?** (Their desire to be honored was the opposite of Jesus' servanthood. Beyond that, they victimized helpless people and were hypocrites in their relationship with God.)

11. In contrast to the selfish Pharisees, Jesus noticed the selfless giving of a poor woman (vss. 41-44). We don't know whether the woman found out that Jesus had seen her, or that she got any earthly reward for her generosity. **What unselfish things have you done during the past week that no one knows about? Would you have done more if you'd known others might hear about it today?**

12. Without talking with her, Jesus knew how much the widow had to live on (vs. 44). **How does it make you feel to know that Jesus knows how much money *you* have? Why?**

Have three kids act out the skit on the reproducible sheet, "The Rest of the Story?" Then discuss: **Are most people like the widow in the real, biblical story, or like the one in the skit? Which widow was "smarter"? Which is more like you? Why?**

THE REST OF THE S·T·O·R·Y?

Cast: Narrator, Widow, Rich Person

NARRATOR: *(Read Mark 12:41-44, then continue with the following dialogue.)* But what if this was . . . the rest of the story?

WIDOW: Hey, wait a minute. What am I doing? I just gave away all the money I had! What am I, crazy?

RICH PERSON: Out of my way, woman. I am about to make a very large donation.

WIDOW: You get out of *my* way. I've got to get my money back. I'm saving up for a new CD player.

RICH PERSON: Why, you're breaking open the collection box! You can't do that!

WIDOW: It was a mistake. I didn't mean to put in *both* copper coins. I'm not a fanatic, you know.

RICH PERSON: Stop it! You're causing a commotion. People will think I've taken your money.

WIDOW: Oh, you love the attention. You'll do anything to get people to look at you. That's why you drop the big drachmas in the offering.

RICH PERSON: I've had it. Here, I'll give you ten copper coins just to go away.

WIDOW: Ten? Wow, what a deal. I should do this again sometime.

RICH PERSON: Now get lost. You're standing in my light. People can't see me.

WIDOW: Wait. Let's see . . . I just got ten coins, so I'll put in one. That's ten percent. See, everybody? I'm just a poor widow, and I'm putting in a *third* coin! I should get a couple of extra verses in Mark 12 for this, huh?

RICH PERSON: Now, *that's* the spirit.

Watch Out!

Prompted by His disciples, Jesus provides some information concerning the "last days" prior to His return. Not all the news is good, but this turbulent time will culminate with the power and glory of God.

(Needed: Assorted prepared signs; prizes [optional])

Make and bring some signs that say things like, "Applause," "Boo/Hiss," "Ha-Ha," "Yee-Hah," "Shhhhhh," etc. Without saying a word, see how far you can prompt your group to action merely by holding up the signs one at a time. Or, if you prefer, form teams and have them compete to see who can respond more loudly to the signs. Then discuss how some signs ("High Voltage," "Detour," "Stop," "No Swimming," etc.) help provide safety and direction if we respond to them. Likewise, responding to "signs" before the return of Jesus will ensure our readiness when He appears.

DATE I USED THIS SESSION _____ GROUP I USED IT WITH _____

NOTES FOR NEXT TIME _____

_____

_____

1. What do you think is the greatest building or monument you've ever seen?

2. When the disciples pointed out how great some of the buildings were in Jerusalem (vss. 1-12), **Jesus didn't seem too impressed. What can we learn from His comments to the disciples?** (As great as our civilization may seem, it won't go on forever. The Jewish temple was destroyed in 70 A.D. by the Romans. Later the Roman Empire fell.)

3. The disciples wanted to know what to watch for as a signal that things were coming to an end (vss. 3, 4). **Do you have any questions of your own about the last days?** (Collect questions and look for answers as you go through the chapter. Deal with unanswered questions in a future meeting.)

4. Can you think of any recent spiritual leaders who have claimed to be Jesus—or His equal—and who have deceived many (vss. 5, 6)? (Some would include in this category Sun Myung Moon of the Unification Church, the Reverend Jim Jones of the People's Temple, New Age "channelers," etc.)

5. What "wars and rumors of wars" (vss. 7, 8) are happening in the world right now? What earthquakes and famines? (Try to have a newspaper on hand and have kids look for relevant articles.)

6. If you're not being arrested and beaten for your faith (vss. 9-11), **how can you apply the promise Jesus makes in verse 11?** (We can count on God to help us as we share our faith with others, take a bolder stand for Him, etc.)

7. Verse 10 says the Gospel must first be preached to all nations. Do you know which nations have heard the Gospel? Do you figure someone else will take care of the fulfillment of this prophecy, or should you have a part in it? What could your role be?

8. Do you think families fight more or less than they did when your parents were kids? What severe family conflicts have been in the news recently (vss. 12, 13)? (Again, try to check a newspaper for stories about family lawsuits, murders, or child or parent abuse.)

9. The world scene just before the return of Jesus will be terrible (vss. 14-25). Even the people still faithful to God ("the elect") are in danger of being misled (vss. 20-22). But what will happen to God's people eventually (vss. 26, 27)? (They'll be taken to heaven—either through death or at Christ's return.) Do you find this comforting, scary, weird, or something else?

10. What are the first signs you notice that show spring is almost here? How about fall? How will we know when to expect the return of Jesus (vss. 28-31)? (While we have no way of forecasting exact days and times, we can notice the signals Jesus gave His disciples and prepare ourselves.)

11. Did Jesus make a mistake in verse 30? After all, the people alive back then have died, and Jesus hasn't come back yet, has He? (According to some commentators, "this generation" could also mean the generation living when the signs begin to occur; or it might refer to the Jewish people as a race; or it might mean all those living in "the church age." Some also think the signs did occur during the first century, but that Jesus' return is yet to come.)

12. Why didn't Jesus give us the precise time of His second coming (vss. 32-37)? (God the Father was in control of the timing. Also, Jesus wants us to be prepared all the time—instead of loafing until the last possible minute.)

The reproducible sheet, "What's Your Sign?" will help kids indicate their readiness for the last days and Jesus' return. As they display their responses, discuss: **If Jesus were to appear here and now, would you be happy—or embarrassed? What would help you feel more ready for the return of Jesus? What three things do you most need to do before Jesus returns?**

SIGN HERE

Which of these signs sum up your feelings about the "end of the age" and the return of Jesus? Circle all that apply to you, and explain why they do. If you can think of another sign that better describes your feelings, draw it at the bottom of the page and be ready to explain it.

Because . . .

Because . . .

Because . . .

Because . . .

Because . . .

Because . . .

Because . . .

Because . . .

Because . . .

Because . . .

Because . . .

Because . . .

Because . . .

MARK 14

A Night to Remember

After being anointed by a woman at Bethany, Jesus spends His final hours with His disciples. They eat the Last Supper, where Jesus predicts the disciples' denial and betrayal. Then He goes to pray in Gethsemane, after which He is arrested and taken before the Jewish court.

(Needed: Assorted craft materials)

Sit in a circle with several craft materials (construction paper, glue, glitter, colored pens, etc.) in the center. Explain: **Let's say you're moving away. What could you make that the rest of us could remember you by?** When everyone finishes, have one person at a time pass around and explain his or her creation. Point out that in this chapter, Jesus establishes the Lord's Supper before He leaves to help us remember that He's going to come again.

DATE I USED THIS SESSION _____ GROUP I USED IT WITH _____

NOTES FOR NEXT TIME _____

_____

_____

1. The Pharisees had been after Jesus for a long time (vss. 1, 2) **and were beginning to close in on Him. If you've ever been chased or otherwise in danger, how did it feel? Do you think Jesus could have, or should have escaped this danger?**

2. What do you think of the woman's gift to Jesus (vss. 3-9)? **Was it a waste or not? What gift could you give Jesus if He appeared here today?**

3. Some people quote the first part of verse 7 ("The poor you will always have with you") as proof that there's no point in trying to help poor people. Based on the whole verse, what do you think Jesus was saying?** (He was saying that honoring Him in person would be possible only for a little while—and after that, there would be plenty of chances to help the poor.)

4. Why did Judas decide to betray Jesus?** (This isn't clear. Various theories have been suggested—that Judas wanted to force Jesus to fight the Romans, that Judas wanted money, that the devil made him do it, etc. He regretted it after Jesus' death, and killed himself.)

5. If you knew you were having your last meal with your friends before you died, would you do anything special? If so, what? How does that compare with verses 12-26?** (Jesus tried to let His friends know what was going to happen, and He instituted the Lord's Supper to give them [and us] a way to remember Him. But He didn't order a special "last meal" or do some of the things we might want to do.)

6. While Judas was planning betrayal, Peter was making promises he wouldn't keep (vss. 27-31). **Which do you think was worse, and why?** (At least Peter, unlike Judas, intended to be faithful to Jesus. Yet both ended up turning their backs on Him.)

7. What's the hardest thing you've ever done because you thought God wanted you to do it? How did you prepare? How does that compare with verses 32-42?** (Jesus enlists the support of believing friends, prepares with fervent prayer, and puts the Father's will above His own. So should we.)

8. Jesus' best friends let Him down three times in the same night (vss. 32-42). **But He still loved them. How do you think He feels about you if you fail Him repeatedly? Why?**

9. When Jesus was approached by the crowd (vss. 43-52), at least one of the disciples was ready to fight. But the disciples hadn't been ready to pray with Him earlier. **When you face a crisis, is it easier for you to take action or to pray? Give some examples.**

10. At Jesus' trial, false witnesses tried to "smear" Jesus, but they couldn't get their stories straight (vss. 55-65). It was Jesus' own statement (vs. 62) that convicted Him. **Which do you think makes more people reject Jesus today: lies about Him, or the truth about Him? Explain.** (Some people never consider the truth about Jesus because lies [that He didn't exist, that what the Bible says about Him can't be trusted] stop them. But others are turned off by the truth—that Jesus is God, that they have sinned and need forgiveness, etc.)

11. Peter dared to follow Jesus to His trial (vss. 53-54). But then he denied even knowing Jesus (vss. 66-72). **Can you think of a way in which you tend to follow Jesus, but only up to a point?** (Examples: Faithfulness on Sunday, but fear of living a Christian life at school; feeling bad about needy people, but not doing anything to help them, etc.)

Use the reproducible sheet, "Once More—with Feelings," to review the emotional rollercoaster of Mark 14. After discussing the feelings and events of the biblical account, spend time exploring kids' own emotional reactions. Then ask: **What will you do with your feelings about what Jesus went through? How could your feelings lead you to follow Him more closely this week?** If possible, have kids pray short prayers expressing their feelings to the Lord.

ONCE MORE WITH FEELINGS

Mark 14 is packed with powerful feelings—and events that pull powerful feelings from us. See whether you can remember who had the following emotions, and why. Then look up the verses to check your answers. Finally, write in how *you* feel about each event—and why.

1. Indignant (vs. 4)
Who felt this way? _____
Why? _____
How do *you* feel about this event?
_____
Why? _____

2. Delighted (vs. 11)
Who felt this way? _____
Why? _____
How do *you* feel about this event?
_____
Why? _____

3. Saddened (vs. 19)
Who felt this way? _____
Why? _____
How do *you* feel about this event?
_____
Why? _____

4. Insistent (vs. 31)
Who felt this way? _____
Why? _____
How do *you* feel about this event?
_____
Why? _____

5. Deeply distressed, troubled, overwhelmed with sorrow (vss. 33, 34)
Who felt this way? _____
Why? _____
How do *you* feel about this event?
_____
Why? _____

6. Scared (vs. 50)
Who felt this way? _____
Why? _____
How do *you* feel about this event?
_____
Why? _____

7. Angry (vss. 63-65)
Who felt this way? _____
Why? _____
How do *you* feel about this event?
_____
Why? _____

8. Weeping (vs. 72)
Who felt this way? _____
Why? _____
How do *you* feel about this event?
_____
Why? _____

MARK 15

The End?

Having been found guilty by a Jewish court, Jesus is sent on to the Romans for sentencing. He is taken before Pilate, mocked by Roman soldiers, crucified, and even then insulted by thieves and onlookers. After His death, He is sealed in a tomb provided by Joseph of Arimathea.

Call up groups of three or four kids to perform impromptu skits. One person in each group should play a superhero or popular tough guy (Superman, Arnold Schwartzenegger in one of his roles, Dirty Harry, a pro wrestler, etc.). The others in the group try to provoke the "hero" to see how much they can get away with before he retaliates. Then explain that the idea of having remarkable power but choosing not to use it appears in Mark 15—in Jesus' refusal to fight those who were killing Him.

DATE I USED THIS SESSION _____ GROUP I USED IT WITH _____

NOTES FOR NEXT TIME _____

_____

_____

1. Jesus had been arrested at night—not during the day when a lot of people would see. Now He is sentenced "very early in the morning" (vs. 1). Why? (Probably so that His supporters couldn't testify for Him or cause trouble.) **How do you suppose that felt for Jesus?** (He probably felt very tired and alone as He stood before His accusers.)

2. Verse 10 gives the real reason why the chief priests had accused Jesus. Why would they envy Him? (He was more popular than they were.) **What do kids do today when they envy someone?** (Try to get the person in trouble, criticize him or her, spread lies—as the religious leaders did to Jesus.)

3. Jesus showed no resistance during this whole time. What things were done to Him which shouldn't have been necessary for a nonthreatening prisoner (vss. 1-20)? (He was bound; held instead of the obviously guilty Barabbas; maligned by the chief priests; flogged by Pilate's men; mocked by the soldiers with a robe and crown of thorns; struck on the head; spit on; and crucified.)

4. If you had Jesus' power and someone tried to do these things to you, what do you think you would do? Why do you think Jesus chose not to act? (When God's will for us includes suffering, we aren't usually as obedient as Jesus was. Jesus knew He must die for the sins of the world, and He didn't buckle under pressure as that time approached.)

5. Jesus wasn't depending on physical strength to get Him through this ordeal. He couldn't even carry His cross (vs. 21). **How do you think He kept going?** (The spiritual bond between Jesus and God the Father provided strength. We should learn to count more on God in times of trouble than in our own abilities.) **Has God ever kept you (or someone you know) going when it would have seemed impossible otherwise?**

6. Of all Jesus' suffering during His crucifixion (vss. 21-32), which do you think was the worst? Why? (Examples: the pain; hanging naked in public; being insulted by self-righteous lowlifes; the loneliness; the rejection.)

7. Have you ever felt as if God had abandoned you? What happened? How could it help to remember that Jesus once felt the same way (vss. 33-37)? (He understands what it's like; His experience shows that there's hope for the future, etc.)

8. Why does it matter that the temple veil was torn (vs. 38)? (The veil separated the Holy Place from the area where "regular" people were allowed to go. Through Jesus' death, we now have direct access to God.) How do you use this "direct access"? How could you use it more?

9. The Roman centurion (vs. 39) seemed to come to a new respect for Jesus after Jesus died. What do you think changed his mind?

10. Is it ever too late to change your mind about Jesus, or to decide to try to do something on His behalf (vss. 37-47)? (While it's never too late to "come around" while we're alive, we have no assurance that we'll be here tomorrow to change our minds. And the sooner we decide to give Jesus our complete loyalty and obedience, the better it will be for us in *this* life.)

The reproducible sheet, "To Die For," encourages kids to think about their response to Jesus' sacrificial death. Discuss the cases one at a time, helping kids to see *before* #4 that another person's sacrifice should lead to our thankfulness and commitment, not just feelings of guilt. After discussion, add an upbeat emphasis—that Jesus died in order for us to "have life, and have it to the full" (John 10:10).

TO DIE FOR

How do you think you would feel and respond in each of the following situations?

1 You and your best friend are goofing off around the railroad tracks. You get one of your $100-a-pair tennis shoes caught in the ties and stubbornly refuse to leave it behind. Your friend is more aware than you are of how close the train is, and rushes over to push you out of the way. In the process, he or she is hit and paralyzed from the neck down for life—but you are just fine.

2 A rare disease requires that you have a heart transplant—if you can find a donor with your uncommon blood type. Just in the nick of time a heart is found and the operation is performed. When you fully recover, you discover that the heart came from a 14-year-old boy who had just been killed in a car accident. Now his parents want to visit you and tell you about their son.

3 A sniper at your school begins shooting randomly. You are in his sights, but at the last moment your favorite teacher jumps in the line of fire and is killed instead of you.

4 You have committed a string of crimes, each of them punishable by death. But a completely innocent man is tortured and killed in your place. Because of His death you will be free and alive forever, entitled to all kinds of benefits—if you only commit to serving Him instead of leading your usual life of disobeying God.

MARK 16

One Impossible Morning

Intending to anoint Jesus' body with spices, several women discover the stone already rolled away from His tomb. An angel explains to them that Jesus has risen and will meet them in Galilee. The news is met with fear and wonder (and doubt on the part of some). Later, Jesus appears, provides some final instructions to the disciples, and ascends into heaven.

(Needed: Items for "Impossible Olympics" stunts [optional])

Option 1: Use the reproducible "Brain Strainer" sheet. After giving kids a couple of minutes, reveal that the items are a bolt, an eye, a letter, a line, a lock, a pan, a weight, and wood. Give them a little more time to try to figure out what the words have in common. Then reveal that all of the words can be preceded by the word "dead" to form commonly used words or phrases. Ask kids what the word "dead" makes them think of. Use this to lead into the Q & A section. *Option 2:* Stage an "Impossible Olympics," challenging kids to do impossible feats like mixing oil and water, squeezing a piece of coal until it becomes a diamond, biting their own noses, etc. Then discuss the "impossible" feat of coming back from the dead.

DATE I USED THIS SESSION _____ GROUP I USED IT WITH _____

NOTES FOR NEXT TIME _____

_____

_____

1. Have you attended many funerals? What have you learned about funeral homes, memorial services, tombstones, and other observations of a person's death? If you avoid these things, why do you?

2. Have you ever wished you could tell someone something after he or she had died—when it was too late? If so, did that change the way you related to other people around you?

3. If you had been a personal friend of Jesus, do you think you would have gone with these women (vss. 1-3)? If not, what excuses might you use? (It's too early, we need to wait until the stone is rolled away, etc.)

4. The women were concerned over who would move the stone. But when they got to the tomb, it was already moved. Have you ever worried about something that might happen, but didn't? What part do you think God played in that?

5. The women were alarmed when they saw the empty tomb and the white-robed man (vss. 4, 5). Why? (They probably thought Jesus' body had been stolen.) What do you think their reaction would have been if they'd found the stone rolled away, but Jesus' dead body still in the tomb?

6. Why doesn't God give us white-robed, heavenly visitors to answer our questions about life? What has He given us instead? (He's given us the Bible, the Holy Spirit, Christian friends, pastors, counselors, etc.) When was the last time you used one of these resources to answer a question you had?

7. The angel wanted the women to take the news to Jesus' disciples *and Peter* (vs. 7). Why was Peter singled out? (Maybe because Peter had denied Jesus, and the Lord knew Peter would be feeling guilty and unworthy of further contact with Jesus.) What special concerns of yours do you want the Lord to be aware of? Do you believe He is?

[*Note:* Mark 16:9-20 is not found in all original manuscripts;

some question its authenticity. Most of it reflects events detailed in other Gospels, but some scholars warn against forming doctrines based on vss. 17, 18.]

8. **Why do you think most of Jesus' disciples doubted His resurrection** (vss. 9-14)**?** (He had tried to prepare them for it, but coming back from the dead takes faith to comprehend and believe. Many people today try to explain it away, too.) **If you'd been one of the Eleven** (vs. 14)**, how would you have explained your doubts to Jesus?**

9. **What's the point of verses 17 and 18? Are we supposed to pick up rattlesnakes and drink poison?** (This passage is a prediction, not an instruction. The apostle Paul was bitten by a poisonous snake and survived [Acts 28:1-6]. The New Testament doesn't record any instances of drinking deadly poison without harm. The point seems to be that God would work miracles and protect His messengers as the Gospel was spread.)

Say: **Peter broke his promises to Jesus, and Jesus died before Peter could apologize. But when Jesus rose, Peter got a second chance to make things right. Think of something you did recently that hurt your relationship with God or with another person. What could you do to make it right? Do you need to ask someone's forgiveness? Peter was given another chance, and in most cases we can have one, too—especially when we fail God.** Let kids share what they've been thinking if they wish, but don't press them. Then pray, thanking God for second chances.

brain strainer

Write the names of the following items in the blanks. Then try to figure out *what all of the words have in common!*

_ _ _ _ _

_ _ _ _

_ _ _ _ _ _ _ _

_ _ _ _ _

_ _ _ _

_ _ _ _ _

_ _ _

_ _ _ _

_ _ _ _ _ _